GUITAR WORLD PRESENTS

THE 100 GREATEST GUITARISTS OF ALL TIME!

From the pages of
GUITAR WORLD
magazine

Edited by
Jeff Kitts and Brad Tolinski

Copyright © 2002 by Hal Leonard Corporation

All rights reserved. No part of this book may be reproduced or utilized in any form or by any means, electronic or mechanical, including photocopying, recording, or any other information storage or retrieval system, without permission in writing from the Publisher, except by a reviewer, who may quote brief passages for review.

Published in cooperation with Harris Publications, Inc., and *Guitar World* magazine
Guitar World is a registered trademark of Harris Publications, Inc.

Cover Photos: Top Left: Dimebag Darrell – Steve Eichner/Retna
Top Right: Jimi Hendrix – Ray Stevenson/Retna
Bottom Left: Kirk Hammett – Jay Blakesberg/Retna
Bottom Right: Neil Young – Michael Putland/Retna

Published by Hal Leonard Corporation
7777 West Bluemound Road
P.O. Box 13819
Milwaukee, WI 53213, USA

Trade Book Division Editorial Offices
151 West 46th Street, 8th Floor
New York, NY 10036, USA

Visit Hal Leonard online at **www.halleonard.com**

Library of Congress Cataloging-in-Publication Data

Guitar world presents 100 greatest guitarists of all time from the pages of Guitar world magazine / edited by Jeff Kitts and Brad Tolinski.--1st ed.
p. cm.
ISBN 0-634-04619-5
1. Guitarists. 2. Popular music--History and criticism. I. Title: 100 greatest guitarists of all time from the pages of Guitar world magazine. II. Title: Guitar world presents one hundred greatest guitarists of all time from the pages of Guitar world magazine. III. Title: One hundred greatest guitarists of all time from the pages of Guitar world magazine. IV. Kitts, Jeff. V. Tolinski, Brad. VI. Guitar world.
ML399 .G86 2002
787.87'092'2--dc21

2002012210

Printed in the United States of America
First edition

10 9 8 7 6 5 4 3 2 1

Table of Contents

PART I:

The 100 Greatest Guitarists of All Time!

The guitar is one of the most flexible vehicles of expression known to man and beast. No instrument appeals to a wider range of personalities—from the anal-retentive classical player to the sociopathic thrasher—and there isn't a single style of music that hasn't been affected by some crazed visionary with a six- or seven-string. (A bold statement, for sure, but we can back it up.)

That's why compiling a list of the 100 greatest guitarists of all time is no picnic. Sure, it's easy to put together a list of the 100 greatest tuba or banjo players (try naming two), but there are so many great guitarists that you'd probably have better luck counting all the "speed versus feel" references that appeared in the pages of *Guitar World* magazine from 1988-92. Nevertheless, we determined souls decided to accept this challenge, even if it led to headaches, arguments and pillow fights.

Now, before you go scanning the list to see if Punky Meadows made the cut (he didn't), let us explain what determined who got a space on the life raft and who got fed to the sharks. While technical ability was important, the candidates' influence on other players held greater weight. Of course, that wasn't the prime consideration, or else we would have called this, "The 100 Most Influential Guitarists." We also considered the guitarists' relevance to today's musician, so their contributions had to be of greater duration than the average Carmen Electra marriage. Originality also ranked high on our list; that's why your brother, who plays a note-perfect version of "Eruption," wasn't considered. Finally, all of the players had to be snappy dressers (extra points were given for exceptionally tight pants).

You may not agree with our selections—in fact, we're counting on it—but we hope that our list will give you some insight into what makes a player a truly great guitarist.

Guitar World, December 2001

Lords of Hard Rock

WES BORLAND

It's just a lot more fun to dress up and look completely bizarre onstage. —Wes Borland

With his black bulging eyes, outrageous stage costumes, freakish makeup and artistic sensibilities, it could be said that Limp Bizkit guitarist Wes Borland is the modern day Ace Frehley—a consummate guitarist with a flair for showmanship and an eye for spectacle. His penchant for the bizarre stems from his background in visual arts (in his spare time, he's a painter, illustrator and sculptor), combined with a healthy interest in science fiction. As for his various stage personas, Borland started off slow—but now he has a vast array of different characters he'll pull out on a given night.

"I like to keep it different," says the Florida native. "I have a bunny suit, a skeleton suit and an oversized kung-fu suit that I wear onstage now. I also have the burnt match character, which is one of my favorites. I go onstage wearing almost nothing. I have underwear and my boots on, and I paint my whole head black—from the neck up—and I have the black contacts. All you can see is these glowing teeth." As for the origin of the horrific black lenses, Borland had them specially made by the people who make the contacts for the sci-fi television series *Babylon Five*. "A lot of people can't look at me," he admits. "They say, 'Oh my god, don't look at me!' "

But while Borland's outlandish stage getups may be what earned him recognition initially, it's his skills as a guitar innovator that have made him one of the premier axemen of the millennium. His playing is wholly untraditional—not a trace of precision soloing, complex neo-classical runs or delicate acoustic fingerpicking can be found on any of Limp Bizkit's three albums: 1997's *Three Dollar Bill,*

Y'all$, 1999's *Significant Other*, or 2000's already quadruple-Platinum *Chocolate Starfish and the Hot Dog Flavored Water*. Instead, Borland has made his mark in the guitar community through creative use of both seven- and six-string instruments and a deep appreciation for in-the-studio wizardry (particularly on his recent solo effort from Big Dumb Face, *Duke Lion Fights the Terror*). He's been known to restring his guitars in unique ways and experiment with all sorts of weird tunings, and layering guitars across the mix is something he's got down to a science. Borland had this to say about the recording of the guitars on *Significant Other*, arguably his band's strongest effort to date:

"On most of the tracks I would have one solid-body electric on either side of the mix, doubled. Then, in the middle, I would have an acoustic guitar going through a Mesa/Boogie Dual Rectifier, full distortion, an Ibanez seven-string acoustic and a Gretsch. Using those two together or separately on different songs just gave a tone that I wasn't getting with any of the solidbodies, guitars that were built to make really heavy distortion sounds. When you bring these acoustic instruments in, the tone is so much more massive. It just adds something."

Traditional guitar aficionados often dismiss Borland as one of those "rap-metal guys," but the truth is that he is at the forefront of the modern generation of players, and will surely serve as the blueprint for the next wave of guitar heroes. Clearly, there's more to Wes Borland than meets the eyes.

- **Equipment:** Ibanez, Paul Reed Smith, Master Guitars four-string semi-acoustic baritone, Fender Jazzmaster, Gretsch hollowbody reissue, Mesa/Boogie and Deizel amps
- **Signature Song:** "Nookie," from Limp Bizkit—*Significant Other* (Interscope, 1999)
- **Classic Album:** Limp Bizkit—*Significant Other*

BRIAN "HEAD" WELCH AND JAMES "MUNKY" SHAFFER

We decided, as a band, to create something together, where we can all step up to the podium and shine and do our own thing.

—Brian "Head" Welch

It's been almost a decade since Korn first blasted out of Bakersfield, California, and in that time the guitar tandem of Brian "Head" Welch and James "Munky" Shaffer has become one of the most formidable pairings of the modern guitar era. With a firm grip on their Ibanez seven-strings, Head and Munky have earned a place among the monsters of rock, detuning their way to the top of the charts and into the hearts of millions of aggro-metal fans the world over.

The music community got its first taste of Korn back in 1992 when the band released its self-titled debut album. Right from the opening sounds of "Blind"—a now classic song which began with a random guitar scrape, a rumbling bass note and singer Jonathan Davis' guttural "Are...you...*readdyyy!?*" followed by one of the heaviest riffs ever created—rockers could sense that Korn's unique, percussive sound was the start of something new. Almost immediately the rock world began buzzing about this new band, and before long, a new heavy metal phenomenon was in full swing—and Korn was right there, leading the way. Today, they are the kings of the modern metal world, bar none.

Over the years Korn have released a number of albums, each one a more focused and refined exercise in extreme heaviness and controlled chaos. The Korn sound is as distinctive as they come, and much of that can be credited to the guitar work of Munky and Head. Their ingenious use of dissonance, distortion and effects are what bring songs like "Got the Life," "Falling Away from Me," "Freak on a Leash" and "A.D.I.D.A.S." to life. And while they have a multitude of pedal effects at their disposal onstage, allowing them to create virtually any sound they wish depending on the song, the guitarists believe the key to their sound lies in the ultra-heavy rumblings of Korn bassist Fieldy. "If you play some of the chords that we do just by themselves, it sounds wrong," says Munky. "But by putting the right bass note behind it—and the right groove—that's how we do it."

- **Equipment:** Ibanez RG7 seven-string guitars, Mesa/Boogie amps, DigiTech XP-100 Whammy Wah
- **Signature Song:** "Got the Life," from Korn—*Follow the Leader* (Epic/Immortal, 1998)
- **Classic Album:** Korn—*Follow the Leader*

ACE FREHLEY

I don't know shit from Shineola. I think that's one of the reasons I'm original.

—Ace Frehley

Ace Frehley may not have changed the way people play the guitar, but he certainly made them want to play. In their mid-to-late-Seventies heyday, Kiss were the most widely recognizable, if not the biggest, band in the world. Millions of starry-eyed, prepubescent boys adopted the spaced-out Frehley as their role model. In fact, it's safe to say that many of today's most prominent rock guitarists—from hard rockers like Pantera's Dimebag Darrell and Rage Against the Machine's Tom Morello to alterna-poppers like Weezer's Rivers Cuomo—would never have picked up a guitar had it not been for the flashy, cosmic and cosmetic Ace.

Frehley prowled Kiss' fire-breathing stage, smoking Les Paul in hand, spinning Keith Richards-inspired rhythm patterns and frenetic blues-box speed licks. And while his warbling vibrato and the primitive cool of his thoughtfully structured, almost geometrically minded solos may not have endeared him to technicians and purists, mothers all across the world will gladly confirm that they had to threaten their sons nightly with dismemberment if they didn't stop copping licks from *Alive!* and do their algebra homework.

- **Equipment:** Gibson Les Pauls; Marshall amps
- **Signature Song:** "Shock Me," from Kiss—*Love Gun* (Mercury, 1977)
- **Classic Album:** Kiss—*Alive!* (Mercury, 1975)

JAMES HETFIELD & KIRK HAMMETT

If you're ever satisfied, the game's over.

—James Hetfield

Metallica's James Hetfield is the greatest rhythm guitarist and songwriter in the history of heavy metal. Ask no questions. Raise no objections. No one can chunk harder, crunch more cruelly or write a meaner riff.

Inspired by such so-called "New Wave of British Heavy Metal" bands as Venom and Diamond Head, as well as the monstrous guitar riffs of Seventies hard rock giants like Black Sabbath and Thin Lizzy, Hetfield forged a sound that would make Metallica one of the most influential bands of the Eighties—the fathers of the entire thrash/speed metal genre.

Interestingly, the group's dizzying tempos were originally the product of pure frustration. "When we realized that our early audiences weren't paying any attention to us, we got really pissed off and decided to try and wake everybody up by playing faster and louder than anybody else," Hetfield recalls.

But Metallica weren't just "faster and louder" than their peers; they were also better. Hetfield's brutal epics were veritable masterpieces, and his unfaltering rhythm chops ensured that they were always delivered with deadly precision. And to top off the lethal mix, lead guitar whiz Kirk Hammett, a fervent disciple of European metal gurus like Michael Schenker and Uli Jon Roth, was always there to deliver whammy bar antics, fleet-footed wah-wah work and carefully structured solos that positively screamed for vengeance.

- **Equipment:** James Hetfield: Gibson and ESP Explorers; Mesa/Boogie Mark II-C+ head. Kirk Hammet: Gibson Flying V, ESP Signature Models; Mesa/Boogie Mark II
- **Signature Song:** "One," from Metallica—*...And Justice for All* (Elektra, 1988)
- **Classic Album:** Metallica—*Master of Puppets* (Elektra, 1986)

TONY IOMMI

I'll try anything to sound heavier.

—Tony Iommi

Grunge, goth, thrash, industrial, death, doom…whatever. None of it would exist without Tony Iommi. A veritable riff-making machine since 1968, Black Sabbath's swarthy master of the guitar is responsible for creating such heavy metal standards as "Iron Man," "Paranoid," "Sweet Leaf" and "War Pigs."

Oddly, Iommi's revolutionary signature sound—deep, ominous and deafening—was the surprise result of a grisly work-related accident that severed the tips of the middle and ring fingers of his fretting hand: "After the accident, I had to develop a new way of playing or quit," recalls Iommi. "First I created a set of thimbles to extend the missing fingertips. Then I switched to light strings because it was difficult to bend heavier strings. Next, I began tuning down as much as three semi-tones to make the playing action even easier. The cumulative effect of these changes on my sound was immediate—it added density and weight. I remember playing 'Black Sabbath' and 'Wicked World' in a club for the first time and everybody just froze."

Iommi's pioneering use of extreme volume was also born out of necessity. "We began turning up because we were fed up with people talking over us while we were playing," Iommi chuckles. "I remember thinking, Screw it, they won't be able to chatter over this!"

- **Equipment:** Gibson SG, John Birch Custom SG, 100-watt Laney, Rangemaster treble booster
- **Signature Song:** "Iron Man," from Black Sabbath—*Paranoid* (Warner Bros., 1971)
- **Classic Album:** Black Sabbath—*Paranoid*

JOE PERRY & BRAD WHITFORD

That's what Aerosmith is—a rock and roll band.

—Joe Perry

Aerosmith guitarists Joe Perry and Brad Whitford do not have an original bone in their Boston born-and-bred bodies, but therein lies their genius. Since their 1973 debut, *Aerosmith*, they've had the goddamn good sense to steal only the good stuff: the Yardbirds' classic two-axe crunch, the Rolling Stones' bluesy vibe, the Beatles' knack for writing instantly memorable guitar hooks and hair and makeup ideas courtesy of New England's finest hookers.

Like master chefs, Perry and Whitford have artfully blended these ingredients and whipped up some of America's very best radio-ready boogie. Even a short list is enough to cause hyperventilation: "Walk This Way," "Dream On," "Toys in the Attic," "Sweet Emotion," "Dude (Looks Like a Lady)" and "Janie's Got a Gun." And while there are many other important songs in Aerosmith's extensive canon, these gems alone are enough to establish the two players as the premier guitar team of the Seventies, Eighties and Nineties.

No, Perry and Whitford are not innovators in the manner of Hendrix, Page or Cobain, but if you ever need someone with a good set of power tools, they are definitely the men to call.

- **Equipment:** Anything and everything.
- **Signature Song:** "Walk This Way," from Aerosmith—*Toys in the Attic* (Columbia, 1975)
- **Classic Album:** Aerosmith—*Toys in the Attic*

SLASH

I've never been one of those guys who wants to solo for longer than he should. My solos complement the song, which is the most important part.
—Slash

In the late Eighties, Slash almost single-handedly slew the shred phenomenon, reminding guitarists that hard rock was invented by Page and Beck, not Paganini and Bach. With his rebellious, street-tough image and down-and-dirty playing style, Slash became a hard rock guitar icon, playing raunchy riffs and aggressive, blues-inspired leads that flattened legions of shred virtuosos like a permed poodle haircut in a rainstorm. "All the advanced rock guitar players made things really complicated," says Slash. "I wasn't intimidated by any of that shit, ever. My basic roots come from a certain hard rock background. You can do a million things with that base."

Slash's playing showed a new generation of guitarists that emotion is as important as chops, paving the way for the emergence of grunge and the Nineties punk rock revival. In the midst of Strat mania in the Eighties, he revived interest in the Les Paul. Although Slash is often pigeonholed as a hard rocker, he has made guest appearances on records by a diverse range of artists, including Iggy Pop, Alice Cooper, Paul Rodgers, Carole King and Michael Jackson.

- **Equipment:** '85 Gibson Les Paul Standard; Marshall 100-watt Jubilee heads; Crybaby wah-wah
- **Signature Song:** "Sweet Child O' Mine," from Guns N' Roses—*Appetite for Destruction* (Geffen, 1987)
- **Classic Album:** Guns N' Roses—*Appetite for Destruction*

Tony Mottram/Retna

Slash

ANGUS & MALCOLM YOUNG

We've been accused of making the same album over and over 12 times. But it's a dirty lie. The truth is, we've made the same album over and over 15 times!

—Angus Young

Dressed like a school boy, AC/DC's spastic lead guitarist Angus Young is hard rock's most exciting and entertaining showman. But when it comes to his guitar playing, the wee Scottish Aussie is one class clown that never fools around. His spotlight-stealing spasms only serve as rocket fuel for his God-given ability to solo with the best of them.

But while Angus was born to rock the house, his stoic brother Malcolm is content to stand in the shadows and lay down the band's unshakable foundation with his pulverizing rhythm guitar. Malcolm's mighty crunch, coaxed from a battered '63 Gretsch Jet Firebird, is, in fact, AC/DC's great secret weapon, the standard against which all power chords are measured.

Although they have done great work before and since, the brothers Young will perhaps always be best known for 1980's *Back in Black*, an all-purpose primer for riff writing and tight, blues-based lead playing.

- **Equipment:** Angus Young: Gibson SG; 100-watt Marshalls. Malcolm Young: '63 Gretsch Jet Firebird; 100-watt Marshalls
- **Signature Song:** "You Shook Me All Night Long," from AC/DC—*Back in Black* (Atlantic, 1980)
- **Classic Album:** AC/DC—*Back in Black*

TOM MORELLO

It took a while for me to realize that I should concentrate on the eccentricities in my playing and find my own voice. —Tom Morello

Tom Morello is hard rock's greatest fusion player—not jazz-fusion a lá Jeff Beck, Al Di Meola and John McLaughlin, but style that marries heavy metal, rap and funk. The wizard of the Whammy Pedal, Morello creates some of the wildest, non-guitarlike sounds imaginable, such as imitating the white noise blur of record-scratching with uncanny precision. His riffs pummel the head like Mike Tyson in his prime, helping drive Rage Against the Machine's politically charged lyrics home.

- **Equipment:** Fender Telecaster, DigiTech Whammy Pedal, Marshall JCM 800 – 2205 with Peavey 4 x 12 cabinets
- **Signature Song:** "Killing in the Name," from *Rage Against the Machine*—Rage Against the Machine (Epic, 1992)
- **Classic Album:** Rage Against the Machine—*Rage Against the Machine*

DIMEBAG DARRELL

Heavy metal is what I'm into. Shit that moves you. Shit that has heart and soul. —Dimebag Darrell

Pantera's "King Dime" is the premier metal guitarist of the new millennium. In an age when most headbangers have packed up their gig bags and moved to greener, grungier pastures, Darrell continues to dish out some of the decade's most brutal and uncompromising thrash. By combining the virtuosity of Edward Van Halen with the hyperactive rhythmic drive of a glue-sniffin' punk guitarist, Darrell has created a style that appeals to classic rockers, fans of death metal and industrial aficionados as well.

- **Equipment:** Washburn signature model; Randall RG 100, Randall Century 200
- **Signature Song:** "Cowboys from Hell," from Pantera—*Cowboys from Hell* (Elektra, 1990)
- **Classic Album:** Pantera—*Vulgar Display of Power* (Elektra, 1992)

JERRY CANTRELL

It requires a lot of confidence when you meet players that you've looked up to for years and end up being friends with them out of mutual respect for each other's music. —Jerry Cantrell

Back before the terms "Seattle sound" and "grunge rock" were part of the universal nomenclature, Jerry Cantrell and his band, Alice in Chains, were burning up the airwaves with "Man in the Box," the hit single from their 1990 debut, *Facelift*. Cantrell's mega-heavy, earth-crushing guitar riffs may have initially pegged him as a metal guitarist, but his dense textures and elegant acoustic playing have shown that he's much more versatile than the average metal or grunge rocker. Expect a new solo album from Cantrell later this year.

- **Equipment:** G&L Rampage, assorted Taylor acoustics; Peavey 5150
- **Signature Song:** "Rooster," from Alice in Chains—*Dirt* (Columbia, 1992)
- **Classic Album:** Alice in Chains—*Dirt*

BILLY CORGAN

There are so many records with loud guitar. I'm trying to figure out how to take the instrument and have it still sound like a guitar, but put you in a different universe. —Billy Corgan

The ultimate Gen-X guitar stylist, Smashing Pumpkins' Billy Corgan gives the impression that his hyperactive brain has nonchalantly absorbed all of rock guitar history. He flits among such styles as mind-warp psychedelia, tender, folky ballads and thrash-metal overkill like a bored teen with a channel switcher. Nineties' rock guitar began with a tug-of-war between shred and grunge, but Corgan found a unique solution to the conflict. He dabbles in both styles, and then some.

- **Equipment:** Fender Stratocaster; Marshall JCM 800; DigiTech Whammy Pedal, Univibe
- **Signature Song:** "Cherub Rock," from Smashing Pumpkins—*Siamese Dream* (Virgin, 1993)
- **Classic Album:** Smashing Pumpkins—*Mellon Collie and the Infinite Sadness* (Virgin, 1995)

The British Giants

JEFF BECK

When he's on, Beck's probably the best there is.

—Jimmy Page

Jeff Beck has been breaking the rules of guitar playing and expanding its horizons ever since he recorded his sitar-influenced lines on "Heart Full of Soul" with the Yardbirds in 1965. He explored psychedelia with the Yardbirds, laid the foundation for heavy metal with the Jeff Beck Group, pioneered jazz-rock fusion as a solo artist in the Seventies and has remained a trend-defying iconoclast in the Eighties and Nineties. "I'm an awkward son of a bitch when it comes to doing the expected," explains Beck.

Rarely relying on effects, Beck has strangled a universe of sounds out of his guitar and amp, playing as if his bare fingers were hardwired to his heart. Utilizing every inch of his ax, Beck can make his guitar sound like a howling beast or a choir of angels. In the last five years, Beck has mastered more styles than most artists attempt over an entire career, assimilating Vietnamese folk music for the *Frankie's House* soundtrack, emulating his hero, rockabilly great Cliff Gallup, with uncanny accuracy on the tribute album *Crazy Legs* (1993) and conjuring the spirit of Jimi Hendrix on a cover of "Manic Depression." Playing with the wild abandon of an adolescent and the passion of a romantic soul, Beck still remains a dangerous radical of the guitar.

- **Equipment:** Fender Stratocaster and Esquire; Marshall 50-watt heads; Rat distortion
- **Signature Song:** "Freeway Jam," from Jeff Beck—*Blow by Blow* (Epic, 1975)
- **Classic Album:** Jeff Beck—*Beckology* (Epic, 1991)

ERIC CLAPTON

The only education I ever really had was finding out about the blues. I mean, I wanted to know everything.

—Eric Clapton

Eric Clapton has successfully reinvented himself dozens of times: Rave-Up King with the Yardbirds; Holy Father of the Anglo-blues with the Bluesbreakers; free-form improvisational genius with Cream; solo rock star; Unplugged balladeer—the chameleon rises to every musical occasion.

By 1965 the 20-year-old Clapton was already considered a legend for his playing with John Mayall's Bluesbreakers. He'd introduced the blues to the masses, interpreting and updating what had been a largely unknown form for the rock generation. Simultaneously, his lush, Les Paul-driven tone marked the absolute turning point in the history of rock, transforming what had been a good-time twang instrument into a vehicle for profound expression.

Ultimately, the most enduring image of this great guitarist will be of Clapton the bluesman, standing on a corner of a stage and exposing his psychic wounds to the masses. It is interesting, though, that, while bluesy in feel, his most memorable songs—"Layla," "Tears in Heaven"—do not utilize the blues structure. While most of Clapton's contemporaries talk reunion and revival, he never retreats behind memories of his "good old days." His *Unplugged* album, which was enormously successful—both for him and acoustic guitar manufacturers—included a radical remake of "Layla." Clapton is one artist who has learned how to grow up.

- **Equipment:** Fender Stratocaster, Martin 00-42; late Fifties Fender Twin
- **Signature song:** "Crossroads," from Cream—*Wheels of Fire* (Polydor, 1968)
- **Classic album:** Derek and the Dominos—*Layla and Other Assorted Love Songs* (Polydor, 1970)

GEORGE HARRISON & JOHN LENNON

I'm not very good technically, but I can make the guitar fuckin' howl and move.
—John Lennon

Few guitarists have influenced the sound and style of rock guitar playing more than John Lennon and George Harrison, particularly their work together in the Beatles from 1962 to '69.

Lennon's driving, scrappy rhythm style was founded on the locomotive pounding of American folk blues—as filtered through the English skiffle craze and rockabilly. He brought a unique chordal sensibility to guitar-based songwriting and arranging, inspired by the eclectic collection of Anglo-American pop, rock, r&b, folk and music hall influences absorbed by him and his writing partner, Paul McCartney (whose guitar contributions to the Beatles were also crucial). As Lennon matured, his proclivity for avant-garde art surfaced in his playing. He was the first pop guitarist to use feedback on a record—the Beatles' 1965 hit, "I Feel Fine." His solo experiments with Yoko Ono probed the jagged frontiers of primal scream art guitar noise, giving a major cue to artists as diverse as Sonic Youth, the Jesus & Mary Chain, Einsturzende Neubauten and Throbbing Gristle.

George Harrison's early love of Carl Perkins and Chet Atkins resulted in his imparting a countryish twang to the Beatles' prototypical Britpop. The "quiet Beatle" became a master of stingingly concise, eight- and 12-bar solos on early Beatles gems like "Can't Buy Me Love" and "A Hard Day's Night." Harrison's gloriously chiming use of the Rickenbacker 12-string inspired both Roger McGuinn (the Byrds) and Pete Townshend (the Who) to pick up the instrument, and helped spawn three decades' worth of "jangle pop" bands. Harrison's late-Sixties studies in Indian classical music and the sitar had a profound impact on his guitar playing, which in turn touched off the psychedelic era in guitar rock. Harrison's example encouraged countless guitarists to explore modal improvisation, micro-tonal string bends and the hypnotic/harmonic possibilities of guitar as a drone instrument. Thanks to him, the electric sitar was invented. Other innovations associated with Harrison are backward guitar, extreme distortion and processing the guitar through an organ Leslie cabinet. By the time of the Beatles' swansong, *Abbey Road* (1969), Harrison had developed the highly lyrical slide guitar style that has become a hallmark of his post-Beatles solo career.

- **Equipment: John Lennon:** Rickenbacker 325, Epiphone Casino; Vox AC30. **George Harrison:** Gretsch Country Gentleman, Rickenbacker 360 12-string; Vox, WEM and Selmer amps
- **Signature Song:** "The End," from the Beatles—*Abbey Road* (Capitol, 1969)
- **Classic Album:** The Beatles—*Revolver* (Capitol, 1966)

JIMMY PAGE

My vocation is more in composition, really, than in anything else—building up harmonies using the guitar, orchestrating the guitar like an army, a guitar army. —Jimmy Page

Arguably the most studied and imitated rock guitarist this side of Jimi Hendrix, Jimmy Page is additionally assured a place in the music's pantheon of greats for his roles as musical director, producer and

Heilemann/Retna

Jimmy Page

all-around guru of Led Zeppelin. Under his shrewd guidance, the band was a powerhouse from the word go, relentless in their bold embrace of such disparate influences as electric blues, Middle Eastern world music and English folk.

The Zeppelin myth is built on a history filled with groupies, private jets, hotel room wreckage and rumored flirtations with the occult. But the Zeppelin magic had everything to do with the indefatigable creative expression of its players and Page's own maverick studio and guitar smarts. To produce work so outlandish and enduring, countless, unglamorous hours of toil were spent coaxing previously unheard-of sounds from crude tube amps while stretching the limits of what Seventies analog recording equipment could reproduce.

From his director's seat, Page brought us intense X-rated features like the orgasmic "Whole Lotta Love," Disney-esque fantasies like the whimsical "The Song Remains the Same" and huge, exotic 70mm epics like "Kashmir" and "Stairway to Heaven." As a guitar chameleon, he produced everything from the tortured screams of "Since I've Been Loving You" to the mysterious acoustic ambience of "Black Mountain Side" (a song that introduced D-A-D-G-A-D tuning to literally millions of dazed and confused followers).

As Page, himself, explained to *Guitar World* in 1993: "Many people think of me as just a riff guitarist, but I think of myself in broader terms. As a musician, I think my greatest achievement has been to create unexpected melodies and harmonies within a rock framework. And as a producer, I would like to be remembered as someone who was able to sustain a band of unquestionable individual talent and push it to the forefront during its working career. I think I really captured the best of our output—the multi-faceted gem that is Led Zeppelin."

- **Equipment:** 1958 Les Paul, Fender Telecaster, Gibson EDS-1275 double-neck; Marshall 100-watt heads
- **Signature Song:** "Stairway to Heaven," from Led Zeppelin—*Led Zeppelin IV* (Atlantic, 1971)
- **Classic Album:** Led Zeppelin—*Led Zeppelin II* (Atlantic, 1969)

KEITH RICHARDS

If I'm a guitar hero, I never really entered the competition—I forgot to fill in the application form. —Keith Richards

The perennial "bad boy" of rock, Keith Richards has exemplified the scruffy English guitar hero—rail thin, messy mop of hair, low-hung guitar and cigarette clenched tightly in the lips—for more than 30 years. The heart and soul and principal guitarist/riff-meister of the Rolling Stones, Richards' signature rhythm guitar style is built primarily from playing Telecasters tuned to open G with the low E string removed (low to high: G, D, G, B, D). With this tuning, Richards has laid down some of the most potent rock ever written—"Honky Tonk Women," "Start Me Up" and "Can't You Hear Me Knocking."

Appropriately nicknamed "Keef Riffhard," Richards synthesized blues and roots-rock influences—in particular, the hard-driving rhythm and lead playing of his biggest hero, Chuck Berry—into the creation of his own signature sound, one that continues to influence many guitarists today.

- **Equipment:** Five-string Fender Telecaster; Fender Twin
- **Signature Song:** "Honky Tonk Women," from the Rolling Stones—*Hot Rocks 1964-1971* (Abkco, 1972)
- **Classic Album:** The Rolling Stones—*Sticky Fingers* (Virgin, 1971)

PETE TOWNSHEND

People like Beck and Hendrix get credit for things he started. Pete was definitely the first to let the guitar feedback, he was the first to break his guitar and he's very good at playing rhythm, too.

—Ritchie Blackmore

One of rock's most powerful rhythm guitarists, Pete Townshend cut a commanding figure onstage slamming crashing chords with sweeping, windmill-like movements of his left arm and smashing his guitars to splinters. But for all of his onstage aggression with the Who, Townshend is also an introspective, emotional guitarist. He plays dramatic, flamenco-inspired 16th-note triplet crescendos, lyrical, melodic lines and lush, arpeggiated rhythm beds, turning the guitar into a virtual orchestra.

After perfecting the three-minute power-pop song on Who singles like "I Can't Explain" and "My Generation," Townshend moved on to more ambitious pursuits and began writing lengthy rock operas such as *Tommy* (1969) and *Quadrophenia* (1973). But throughout all of his musical pursuits, his passionate guitar playing has remained a focal point, conveying as much of the songs' meaning as his insightful lyrics.

- **Equipment:** Gibson SG Special; Hiwatt 100-watt heads
- **Signature Song:** "Won't Get Fooled Again," from the Who—*Who's Next* (MCA, 1971)
- **Classic Album:** The Who—*Who's Next*

NIGEL TUFNEL

If you put a hungry ferret in your trousers, he'll run around. You'd be surprised at the energy.

—Nigel Tufnel

It is man's bitter fate that he must forever argue over who is the best guitarist on this sullied earth. But all men agree that Spinal Tap's Nigel Tufnel thinks he is the greatest. "Let those boys like Beck and Clapton fight it out with each other. Let me watch and laugh," says Tufnel suavely.

Too fast for love, hotter than hell, and thicker than a brick, Tufnel's unique take on hard rock has always been inimitable. "No one plays like him," says Spinal Tap frontman David St. Hubbins. "No one even tries."

The guitarist's often-protracted solos, like bowel movements from hell, are dense, gut-wrenching and fluid. "It's not the amount of notes you play, but if you're thinking about them after you played them," says Tufnel philosophically. "Can you remember what you played? If you can't, why did you play it? It becomes a thinking man's game...and who wants to muck about with that?"

- **Equipment:** Too many guitars to mention, specially modified Marshall amps
- **Signature Song:** "(Tonight I'm Gonna) Rock You Tonight," from Spinal Tap—*This is Spinal Tap* (Polydor, 1983)
- **Classic Album:** Spinal Tap—*Shark Sandwich* (Polymer, 1974)

Fallen Heroes

DUANE ALLMAN

There's a lot of different forms of communication, but music is absolutely the purest one, man. There's nothing that could ever be bad about playing music. —Duane Allman

Duane Allman and the Allman Brothers Band inspired hordes of unwashed Southern boys to put down their shotguns and Bud longnecks and pick up guitars and bottlenecks, giving birth to the "Southern rock" genre. But whereas many of the players who followed in his footsteps have gained notoriety for their seemingly endless solos (think "Freebird" or "Green Grass and High Tides"), Allman's immaculate, improvised melodic lines, soaring, weeping slide and dual-guitar interplay with Dickey Betts remain as potent and fresh as the best moonshine liquor.

Allman often alternated between slide and standard playing techniques, combining the two approaches seamlessly with his fluid tone and immaculate intonation (the song "Mountain Jam" is a fine example of this). "I heard Ry Cooder playing slide, and I said, 'Man, that's for me,'" said Allman, who employed a small Coricidin medicine bottle on his ring finger for his bottleneck work. Allman also collaborated with Eric Clapton on the timeless classic "Layla," writing the song's signature lick and playing the ethereal slide parts that dominate the tune. Allman died in a motorcycle accident in 1971, but no guitarist since has made such a powerful and immediate impact on slide guitar.

- **Equipment:** Gibson Les Paul Standard, Gibson SG; 50-watt Marshall amp, Fender Princeton
- **Signature Song:** "One Way Out," from the Allman Brothers Band—*Eat a Peach* (Polydor, 1972)
- **Classic Album:** The Allman Brothers Band—*At Fillmore East* (Polydor, 1971)

KURT COBAIN

I just can't believe that anyone would start a band just to make the scene and be cool and have chicks. —Kurt Cobain

Although it's tempting to imagine Kurt Cobain as just a symbol of alterna-rock angst, the power and ingenuity of his playing proves that there was more than "teen spirit" at work in his music. Cobain grew up in Aberdeen, Washington, where his initial points of reference were hard rock staples like AC/DC, Led Zep, Kiss and Cheap Trick. In 1980, he discovered punk, and his musical course was set.

Never a technical player, Cobain rarely relied on flash, preferring to make his point through dynamics instead, fleshing out his songs with judicious use of distortion and feedback. Even his "solos" tended to be self-effacing in the extreme; the guitar break in "Teen Spirit," for example, merely reprised the vocal line. But Cobain's deft use of harmony and lean, tuneful sense of line more than made up for any lack of chops, shoring up the songs so exquisitely that it was easy to overlook how elegant his playing was.

- **Equipment:** Left-handed Fender Mustang, Ferrington custom; Mesa/Boogie amps
- **Signature Song:** "Smells Like Teen Spirit," from Nirvana—*Nevermind* (DGC, 1991)
- **Classic Album:** Nirvana—*Nevermind*

JIMI HENDRIX

It's the most psychedelic experience I ever had, going to see Hendrix play. When he started to play, something changed; colors changed, everything changed.

—Pete Townshend

The ultimate guitar hero, Jimi Hendrix remains one of the most influential forces in rock. Pulling unprecedented sounds out of his instrument, Hendrix challenged guitarists to explore a wild new world of tones and textures, dazzling and confounding guitar greats like Eric Clapton, Jeff Beck and Pete Townshend, who still revere Hendrix as if he were the Messiah. Other players before him might have experimented with feedback and excessive distortion, but Hendrix turned those practices into an art form. He was the first player to use the whammy bar as an instrument unto itself, making his guitar talk, scream and howl.

"The music I might hear I can't get on the guitar," said Hendrix. "It's a thing of just laying around daydreaming or something. If you pick up your guitar and try to play it, it spoils the whole thing."

Judging from the moans of ecstasy, lashing flames of fire and vastness of space that Hendrix actually managed to evoke with his instrument, the music that he heard in his head must have been truly godlike. The recording studio was as much Hendrix's instrument as the guitar, and he pioneered effects such as backward tracking, flanging and phasing in his efforts to make the guitar communicate the sounds he imagined.

Hendrix's style was based in the blues, but he borrowed from a wealth of sources, including soul, pop, jazz and classical. "I'd like to get something together, like with Handel and Bach and Muddy Waters, a flamenco type of thing," Hendrix remarked. "If I could get that sound, I'd be happy." He challenged conventional notions of pop music with his psychedelic, multi-tracked guitar orchestras, inspiring bands like the Beatles and the Rolling Stones to compose some of their finest work.

Hendrix died in 1970 at the tender age of 27 and well before his prime.

- **Equipment:** Fender Stratocaster; 100-watt Marshall stack; Vox wah, Dallas-Arbiter Fuzz Face, Uni-Vibe, Octavia
- **Signature Song:** "Machine Gun," from Jimi Hendrix—*Band of Gypsys* (Capitol, 1970)
- **Classic Album:** The Jimi Hendrix Experience—*Are You Experienced?* (Reprise, 1967)

RANDY RHOADS

He was too good to last. —Ozzy Osbourne

In 1980 metal was officially dead and singer Ozzy Osbourne's career was in shambles. The vocalist had departed from Black Sabbath under dubious circumstances and was considered to be "dangerously unstable." Then, like a bolt from the blue, Ozzy found Randy Rhoads, a gifted guitarist who had earned cult status with the L.A. glam band Quiet Riot.

Along with Van Halen, Ozzy's new band resurrected heavy rock and ushered in a new era of guitar heroes. Rhoads was initially accused of being an Eddie Van Halen clone, but it soon became evident that he had something very new to offer. His advanced knowledge of music theory and classically influenced melodies starkly contrasted with Edward's intuitive, blues-based approach.

Both *Blizzard of Ozz* (1981) and *Diary of a Madman* (1981) offered staggering, new possibilities to rock guitarists, and Rhoads' potential seemed limitless. The extent of his genius will never be known, as in March 1982, Randy was killed in a tragic plane accident in Orlando, Florida.

- **Equipment:** 1981 Custom Jackson; 100-watt Marshall, MXR Equalizer
- **Signature Song:** "Flying High Again," from Ozzy Osbourne—*Diary of a Madman* (Jet/Epic, 1981)
- **Classic Album:** Ozzy Osbourne—*Blizzard Of Ozz* (Jet/Epic, 1981)

STEVIE RAY VAUGHAN

When most of us play a 12-bar solo, we play maybe two choruses and the rest is all repetition. Stevie Ray wasn't like that. The longer he played, the better he played.
—B.B. King

He seemed to come out of nowhere—a mysterious Texan who played an exciting, progressive style of blues which paid deep homage to tradition while managing to keep an eye on the future. One part Albert King, one part Jimi Hendrix and one part a composite of an entire universe of rock, jazz and other blues artists, Stevie Ray fused his various rootsy selves into an original whole and almost single-handedly demonstrated that not only was the blues alive and kicking, but that it remained a viable vehicle for self-expression in the Eighties and Nineties.

Discovered in a Dallas club by Mick Jagger and Keith Richards in 1982, Vaughan and his band, Double Trouble, were the first act ever to perform the Montreux Jazz Festival without a record contract. Soon after the Festival, Vaughan gained national exposure playing on David Bowie's *Let's Dance* (EMI, 1983), and was subsequently signed to Epic Records by veteran A&R man John Hammond. Vaughan followed the release of his scorching debut, *Texas Flood* (1983), with 18 months of touring, at the end of which he and Double Trouble released *Couldn't Stand the Weather* (1984) and became blues superstars.

Hammond, who also played a key role in the careers of such American music legends as Count Basie, Charlie Christian, Bob Dylan, Aretha Franklin and Bruce Springsteen, put it best: "Stevie's the true kind of creative force that one looks for but rarely finds. I automatically compare him to Robert Johnson because Stevie's got that unique passion."

At the height of his career, Vaughan died in a helicopter accident on August 27, 1990. On hearing of his death, blues great Buddy Guy commented, "Stevie did for us what Muddy Waters did. He put the blues over, and then he came back and got us. We'll all miss him."

- **Equipment:** Stratocaster with a '59 body '61 neck; Fender Vibroverb and 150-watt Dumbles; Ibanez Tube Screamer
- **Signature Song:** "Pride and Joy," from Stevie Ray Vaughan and Double Trouble—*Texas Flood* (Epic, 1983)
- **Classic Album:** Stevie Ray Vaughan and Double Trouble—*In Step* (Epic, 1989)

Robert Matheu/Retna

Stevie Ray Vaughan

The Bluesmen

REVEREND GARY DAVIS

When I first heard the Reverend, that just blew everything else away. That's all I listened to for three years.

—Jorma Kaukonen

Born around the turn of the century in South Carolina, Reverend Gary Davis moved to North Carolina where he developed a spectacularly virtuosic playing style grounded in ragtime, gospel and blues. The few recordings he made in 1935 and 1949 showcase the blazing thumb-and-index fingerpicking and improvisational gifts that years later would make him among the most admired and emulated acoustic bluesmen.

Davis enjoyed his greatest success during the folk boom of the Sixties, when he recorded some brilliant solo albums and appeared at the Newport Folk Festival. An active teacher, Davis taught many would-be bluesmen, most of them young whites, the intricacies of blues and ragtime picking. His impact on second-generation guitarists is most dramatically evident in the acoustic guitar playing of Jorma Kaukonen, who as a solo artist and especially with Hot Tuna recorded and popularized such Davis classics as "Hesitation Blues," "Death Don't Have No Mercy" and "I Am the Light of This World."

- **Equipment:** Gibson J-200, Bozo 12-string
- **Signature Song:** "Candyman," from Reverend Gary Davis—*Pure Religion & Bad Company* (Folkways/Smithsonian, 1991)
- **Classic Album:** Reverend Gary Davis—*The Complete Early Recordings of Reverend Gary Davis* (Yazoo, 1994)

BUDDY GUY

What he does is just plain raw. I don't mean raw without finesse. I mean raw, like raw can be real gentle as easily as it can be bare wires.

—Stevie Ray Vaughan

Louisiana-born, Chicago-bred Buddy Guy is at the commercial zenith of his career, recording for a major label, touring the world, making guest appearances with the likes of Eric Clapton and hobnobbing with the stars. His contributions to blues guitar are widely recognized, especially as a kind of "missing link" between the modern, West Side Chicago-style blues and later blues-based rock of the Jimi Hendrix persuasion. Guy often sounds like a hybrid of the two, playing blues phrases and inflections but with a rapid-fire attack and expansive soloing more characteristic of rock.

Guy moved to Chicago in 1957, gradually earning a reputation for his guitar-playing abilities and drawing choice assignments as a sideman, playing on sessions for the Chess and Cobra labels. In the mid Sixties, he teamed up with harmonica player Junior Wells in what became one of the longest-running blues partnerships.

As a solo artist, Guy was a relatively late bloomer. Only in the last decade has substantial recognition come his way from outside the core blues community. Even among blues fans, there are two schools of thought about Guy. Some listeners tend to find his playing too frantic, the jacked-up intensity too unrelenting to be truly effective. But while there's no denying that Guy is flashy and that his playing often seems faster than his thinking, there's also no denying Guy's extraordinary prowess on his instrument, and for many he is and will remain *the* blues guitarist.

- **Equipment:** Fender Stratocaster, Fender 4 x 10 Bassman
- **Signature Song:** "Leave My Girl Alone," from Buddy Guy—*The Complete Chess Studio Recordings* (Chess, 1992)
- **Classic Album:** Buddy Guy—*The Complete Chess Studio Recordings*

Simon Meaker/Retna

Buddy Guy

JOHN LEE HOOKER

The blues don't have no changes. The hard blues, the natural blues, the soul blues, they ain't got no changes. It's not in the book. —John Lee Hooker

Even in blues, an idiom rich in personal, idiosyncratic stylings that frequently bend, break or ignore "the rules," John Lee Hooker is an anomaly. Hooker was born in 1920 near Clarksdale, Mississippi, birthplace of Muddy Waters, among many others, but his music sounds nothing like the work of any other Delta bluesmen. Possessing a rocking, boogie-based drive, Hooker's deeply emotional music is utterly original.

Hooker basically follows his own muse's prompting. If his discursive, often irregularly structured, almost freeform music-making is reminiscent of anyone on record, it is the fiercely independent Louisiana bluesman Robert Pete Williams. Hailing from the same area as Hooker's father, Williams taught John Lee the celebrated "boogie" style on which much of his success rests.

Hooker may have partly carried on a hitherto-unrecorded regional tradition from Louisiana. But hearing his radical transformations of tunes associated with pianist Amos Milburn, east coast ragtime guitarist Blind Boy Fuller and even swing bandleader Glenn Miller ("I'm in the Mood"), one realizes that Hooker is also one of a kind.

That is evident on his first record, "Boogie Chillen," which made it to number one on the r&b charts in 1949. It was an astonishing record, often called "primitive" for the distorted, heavily jacked-up amplified acoustic guitar sound and the emphatic backbeat of Hooker's feet stamping on a sheet of plywood. "Boogie Chillen" has inspired a disparate group of musicians from Bo Diddley and Sleepy LaBeef to Bonnie Raitt and the Rolling Stones.

Music stars like Santana and Los Lobos have collaborated with Hooker, but playing with him is a privilege not granted the average mortal, even if the mortal is a fairly accomplished guitarist. That's because Hooker goes his own way, making each verse longer or shorter than 12 bars as he feels it.

- **Equipment**: Stella acoustic with a pickup, Gibson Les Paul, Epiphone Sorrento; Fender Twin
- **Signature Song:** "Boogie Chillen," from John Lee Hooker—*The Ultimate Collection 1948-1990* (Rhino, 1991)
- **Classic Album:** John Lee Hooker—*The Ultimate Collection 1948-1990*

BLIND LEMON JEFFERSON

The father of country blues, he influenced generations of guitarists—none of whom could successfully imitate his playing.

—Stefan Grossman

Blind Lemon Jefferson occupies a unique position in the history of the blues. Born in Texas around 1897, blind from birth, Jefferson was the first self-accompanied, guitar-playing male bluesman to enjoy recording success. (Before Jefferson recorded his first hits, blues had been dominated commercially by "classic," vaudevillian blueswomen such as Ma Rainey and Bessie Smith.)

In 1926, Jefferson's first recordings became runaway best-sellers among black music-lovers, and the classics and hits—"See That My Grave Is Kept Clean," "Black Snake Blues," "Matchbox Blues" (the model for the Carl Perkins/Beatles hit "Matchbox") and others—followed in rapid succession.

Rather than accompany his vocals with a steady rhythm or strummed chords, Jefferson tended to use his guitar for rambling, discursive fills between vocal lines, even if the underlying rhythm was compromised. This approach did not immediately register in the Mississippi Delta or the Southeast, but in Texas, Jefferson was widely imitated, and many of his followers carried on his penchant for improvising single-note lines. The approach proved even more adaptable when Jefferson's former "lead boy," Aaron "T-Bone" Walker, adapted it to the electric guitar.

By the time he died in 1929 (according to one rumor, he died in a Chicago blizzard; according to another, he was poisoned), Jefferson's guitar playing, keening tenor vocals and songs had influenced white country music and western swing as well as blues.

- **Equipment:** unknown
- **Signature Song:** "See That My Grave Is Kept Clean," from Blind Lemon Jefferson—*King of the Country Blues* (Yazoo, 1990)
- **Classic Album:** Blind Lemon Jefferson—*King of the Country Blues*

ALBERT KING

Albert King can blow Eddie Van Halen off the stage with his amp on standby.
—Joe Walsh

Albert King's influence on rock guitarists probably eclipsed that of any other blues guitarist for a considerable period during the middle and late Sixties. Born Albert Nelson in 1923, in Indianola, Mississippi, he acquired his first guitar in the late Thirties. Though he first recorded in 1953, Nelson really began to come into his own after moving to St. Louis in the late Fifties. There he developed a guitar style which, while roughly conforming to the T-Bone Walker/B.B. King format of vocals answered by single-note lead lines, had a much heavier feel.

With a sound as brawny as his bulldozer driver's physique, Albert's guitar seemed to ooze from note to note like a slowly spreading oil slick. Though he played exclusively with his fingers, the liquid quality of his lines recalls some of the music's leading slide stylists, most notably Robert Nighthawk. The style was evident on early-Sixties sides Albert made for Bobbin and King, but everything really came together beginning in 1966 when he signed with Stax in Memphis. Recording with backing by house rhythm section Booker T. and the M.G.'s, Albert combined heavily amplified blues/rock guitar leads with drummer Al Jackson's funky beats in a wholly natural, organic manner. The results are King's lasting legacy: "Born Under a Bad Sign," "Laundromat Blues," "Cross Cut Saw" and so on.

Eric Clapton pinched a great deal of Albert's "Cross Cut Saw" solo for his own guitar solo on Cream's "Strange Brew," and in fact Cream's entire *Disraeli Gears* album is known in certain circles as "the Albert King tribute" for its extensive borrowings. King's later recordings sometimes suffered from production problems, but there were triumphs as well, and King continued to play inspirationally at live gigs right up to the time of his death in 1992.

- **Equipment:** Gibson Flying V; Acoustic and Roland JC-120 amps
- **Signature Song:** "Born Under a Bad Sign," from Albert King—*Born Under a Bad Sign* (Stax, 1967)
- **Classic Album:** Albert King—*Born Under a Bad Sign*

B.B. KING

He's the father of the squeezing of the string of the electric guitar. The original 'Sweet Little Angel' made me cry when I first heard it.

—Buddy Guy

B.B. King is one of those rare musicians who has shaped his chosen musical idiom so thoroughly, it's near-impossible to imagine what it would have sounded like without him. King's dominance of modern electric blues is in some ways reminiscent of Charlie Parker's ascendancy over modern jazz. It's a telling measure of these musicians' impact that their work provided the basic instrumental vocabulary and performing format for an entire generation of players.

In blues, B.B.'s penetrating finger vibrato, his gorgeously rounded tone and speech-like phrasing can be heard reflected, more or less literally, in the playing of everyone from Buddy Guy and Otis Rush to Eric Clapton and Michael Bloomfield. B.B.'s remakes of tunes drawn from earlier blues tradition always seem to become the definitive versions. And the sort of gospelish vocal fervor and stinging call-and-response between vocal and guitar that B.B. popularized is known, not as "King style," but simply as the way modern blues is played.

As for where it's played, King took the blues uptown, out of the juke joints and the Southern chitlin circuit and into the cultural mainstream of major-label pop hits, television commercials and lucrative engagements in rock halls, arenas and Las Vegas.

King has recorded more than 70 albums in his lifetime, and at 76 years old he still enjoys an active career, performing hundreds of concerts every year.

- **Equipment:** Gibson ES-355; Fender Twin Reverb, Gibson Lab Series amp
- **Signature Song:** "The Thrill is Gone," from B.B. King—*Anthology* (MCA, 2000)
- **Classic Album:** B.B. King—*Live at the Regal* (MCA, 1965)

FREDDIE KING

I was interested in white rock and rollers until I heard Freddie King—then I was over the moon.
—Eric Clapton

Freddie King grew up far from the Mississippi Delta milieu that nurtured the other Kings of blues guitar, Albert and B.B. Born in Gilmer, Texas, in 1934, Freddie King was exposed to the likes of T-Bone Walker and Lightnin' Hopkins, and he was already playing Texas-style guitar, with a rural flavor, when he headed to Chicago at age 16. In the windy city, King acquired more down-home influences, including valuable tutoring from local guitar masters Jimmy Rogers and Eddie Taylor.

By 1950, when he signed with King Records in Cincinnati, Freddie had combined melodic influences with the rougher edges and raw excitement of the Delta and Chicago styles. At the same time, he was capable of sustaining guitar solos that were longer, more logically organized and thematically coherent than those of most other blues-trained players. This ability, and the sensitive collaboration of pianist/arranger Sonny Thompson, enabled King to enjoy a kind of dual-recording career. On the one hand, he put out vocal blues, with his dark-hued, smokey vocals up front and the guitar answering his phrases. And he put out instrumentals, among them "Hideaway," "The Stumble," the outstanding country and western-derived "Remington Ride" and "San-Ho-Zay," which were covered in Britain by John Mayall, Chicken Shack and others. Eric Clapton says Freddie King was originally his primary influence, and this is certainly clear on recordings Clapton made before his romance with Albert King's style in the late Sixties.

King's career benefited from the unsolicited testimonials of his rock star admirers when he signed with Atlantic's Cotillion label in 1969, then with Leon Russell's Shelter label in 1971. From there he went to RSO, a label that was run by Clapton's then-manager. In 1976, his unexpected death cut short a career that was just showing signs of turning him into a national icon.

- **Equipment:** 1954 Gibson Les Paul, Gibson ES-355; Fender Twin Reverb, Fender Quad Reverb
- **Signature Song:** "The Stumble," from *Hideaway: The Best of Freddie King* (Rhino, 1993)
- **Classic Album:** *Hideaway: The Best of Freddie King*

HUBERT SUMLIN

I knew Howlin' Wolf was one of the greats. I wanted to push him over the top.
—Hubert Sumlin

Combing through Hubert Sumlin's recordings of the past 20 years in search of the guitarist's sometimes-elusive spark of genius can be a frustrating experience. Sumlin has rarely been consistent. The wrenched, shattering bursts of notes, sudden cliff-hanger silences and daring rhythmic suspensions that made his work with Howlin' Wolf so dramatic and riveting seemed to consciously court chaos and sometimes fell headlong into it.

But Sumlin's lead guitar work with Wolf (roughly from 1955 until the singer's death in 1976) was definitive. There's nothing else quite like it in blues; somehow, the ferocious voodoo of Wolf's music inspired Sumlin to outdo himself in an utterly personal form of expression.

Sumlin and Wolf's relationship went back years. Born in the Mississippi Delta near Greenwood, Sumlin was a teenager when he first met Wolf in the Forties. Wolf and other musicians in his circle took a liking to the youngster and tutored him. After Wolf moved to Chicago and parted ways with his longtime guitarist Willie Johnson in the mid Fifties, he brought the still-youthful Sumlin into the group. They gigged all over Chicago and toured the deep South frequently, and their extraordinary collaboration was fortunately preserved on a series of stunning Chess singles: "Evil," "Forty Four," "Smokestack Lightnin' " (with Willie Johnson and Hubert), "Wang Dang Doodle," "Back Door Man," "Spoonful," "The Red Rooster," the epochal proto-heavy metal "I Ain't Superstitious," "Tail Dragger," "300 Pounds of Joy," "Killing Floor" (Sumlin and Buddy Guy!) and many more. Wolf used to call Sumlin his "son"; you'll be calling him "maestro."

- **Equipment:** Gibson Les Paul, Gibson ES-335; Fender amplifiers
- **Signature Song:** "Killing Floor," from Howlin' Wolf—*Greatest Hits* (Chess, 1986)
- **Classic Album:** Howlin' Wolf—The Chess Box (Chess, 1991)

T-BONE WALKER

He was the first man that made the electric guitar popular.

—John Lee Hooker

T-Bone Walker electrified the blues like a lightning bolt from the heavens. Infusing the blues with a sophisticated, uptown attitude, Walker helped redirect the course of the music, taking it from juke joints and roadhouses to swank nightclubs and large theaters. Favoring swing rhythms and big band accompaniment, Walker blended jazz and the blues and became a seminal figure in the development of urban blues and early rock and roll.

"T-Bone Walker was to the blues what Charlie Christian was to jazz," says Walker's biographer Helen Oakley Dance. "Between them, they effectively made the electric guitar a dominant voice not only in their own particular fields, but in the popular music of the whole western world."

Born in Dallas in 1910, Walker grew up steeped in the blues. At age eight, he guided Blind Lemon Jefferson around the city's streets; Huddie "Lead Belly" Ledbetter was a frequent visitor at his mother's house. In the mid Thirties, Walker spent time in Oklahoma City jamming with another young guitarist, Charlie Christian, and learning from Christian's sophisticated teacher, Chuck Richardson, who encouraged T-Bone's jazzier harmonic tendencies.

After moving to Los Angeles at the beginning of the Forties, he worked as a jazz guitarist, and as a featured performer with Les Hite's Los Angeles Cotton Club Orchestra, he also experimented with amplification, which was still in its infancy. With Hite, Walker recorded "T-Bone Blues," his first electric guitar featured on disc, in 1940. Classics like "Mean Old World" and "Call It Stormy Monday" followed. Between 1940 and the mid Fifties, when rock and roll temporarily eclipsed blues in the black community, he made the records that comprise his lasting legacy, the best of which were on Black & White, Capitol and Imperial. After spending much of the Sixties and early Seventies performing widely in Europe and at clubs and festivals around the world, Walker died in 1975.

- **Equipment:** Gibson ES-250, Gibson ES-5; Gibson EH-150 amp, Fender 4 x 10 Bassman
- **Signature Song:** "Call It Stormy Monday," from *Blues Masters: The Very Best of T-Bone Walker* (Rhino, 2000)
- **Classic Album:** T-Bone Walker—*The Complete Capitol/Black & White Recordings* (Capitol, 1995)

MUDDY WATERS

The first guitarist I was aware of was Muddy Waters. I heard one of his records when I was a little boy, and it scared me to death.

—Jimi Hendrix

Muddy Waters, born McKinley Morganfield in 1915 in Rolling Fork, Mississippi, learned his music from the best the Delta had to offer; Son House and Robert Johnson were his primary inspirations. By 1941–42, when folklorist Alan Lomax found him on a plantation near Clarksdale, Muddy was the proprietor of a rough-and-tumble juke joint, as well as its supplier of white lightning. Muddy's recordings for Lomax, issued on *The Complete Plantation Recordings* (MCA, 1993), were acoustic country blues, robust and haunting but also squarely in the older Delta tradition.

After Waters moved to Chicago in 1943, he took up electric guitar in order to be heard over the noise in the taverns. Recording for Chess beginning in 1947, he used his guitar, amp and bottleneck to create a shivery, almost supernaturally vivid sound with help from Leonard Chess and his recording engineers. Meanwhile, in the taverns, Muddy was assembling one of the very first truly electric bands, with second guitarist Jimmy Rogers and the virtuoso and innovator of the amplified harmonica, Little Walter. Once this group began recording with Muddy, they aced one classic after another: "Louisiana Blues," "Long Distance Call," "Honey Bee," "Hoochie Coochie Man," "Mannish Boy" and on and on.

As the Fifties ended and rock and roll all but eclipsed the popularity of the blues, Muddy found a new audience in England, where his first concert tours were a crucial inspiration for the Sixties r&b boom. Muddy was soon performing for white rock audiences at home as well as abroad, and in later years frequently played in stadiums with the likes of Eric Clapton.

Though he played slowly and didn't sound like a virtuoso, Muddy's unique feel, especially on slide, his self-described "delay timing" and ear for microtonal pitch have rarely been effectively imitated. Waters had been intending to write an autobiography but died peacefully in his sleep in 1983 before he could complete this work. Wherever the blues goes from here, there isn't likely to be another Muddy Waters.

- **Equipment:** Fender Telecaster, Gibson Les Paul; Fender Super Reverb
- **Signature Song:** "Hoochie Coochie Man," from Muddy Waters—*The Chess Box* (Chess, 1989)
- **Classic Album:** Muddy Waters—*The Chess Box*

David Redfern/Retna

Muddy Waters

Virtuosos

RITCHIE BLACKMORE

I'm not good enough, technically, to be a classical musician. I lack the discipline. When you're dealing with classical music, you have to be rigid. I'm not a rigid player. I like to improvise.
—Ritchie Blackmore

"Smoke on the Water." There is far more to Ritchie Blackmore than The Riff—the one every would-be guitarist from Timbuktu to Taylor, Michigan, aspires to learn. In his late Sixties and Seventies heyday, Ritchie Blackmore raised the bar several notches for what it meant

Michael Putland/Retna

Ritchie Blackmore

to be a guitar hero by experimenting with classically inspired lines. "I found the blues too limiting," says Blackmore. "I'd always thought—with all due respect to B.B. King—that you couldn't just play four notes. Classical, on the other hand, was always too disciplined. I was always stuck between the two, stuck in a musical no-man's land."

Blackmore's Bach-like arpeggios and Mozart-influenced solos, such as his lead on "Highway Star," opened up new avenues of exploration for many players to follow, including Brian May, Edward Van Halen, Yngwie Malmsteen, Michael Schenker and Steve Morse.

- **Equipment:** Fender Stratocaster; Marshall Major 200-watt heads
- **Signature Song:** "Highway Star," from Deep Purple—*Machine Head* (Warner Bros., 1972)
- **Classic Album:** Deep Purple—*Machine Head*

AL DI MEOLA

Guitar albums are just not appreciated by non-guitarists. My goal is to go over the top, because an artist wants his music to appeal to everyone.

—Al Di Meola

Al Di Meola gained notoriety first as a member of Return to Forever, Chick Corea's jazz-fusion ensemble, and later for the fiery, passionate playing on his early solo albums. His incredibly fast and precise palm-muted lines and thick, distorted tone made him a favorite among rock guitarists, many of whom had their first exposure to jazz through him.

A versatile instrumentalist, Di Meola has developed a diverse repertoire that encompasses classical, flamenco and Latin music, greatly expanding both his and his audience's notions of what defines jazz guitar. Even when playing his blindingly quick lines, Di Meola displays an admirable sense of melody, emotion and drama.

In the early Eighties, he teamed up with two other exemplary guitarists, John McLaughlin and Paco De Lucia, for a highly successful and critically acclaimed all-acoustic tour that was documented on the best-selling *Friday Night in San Francisco* (1980) album. Lately, Di Meola has focused on acoustic music and released a pair of albums influenced by the work of accordionist Astor Piazzolla.

- **Equipment:** 1971 Gibson Les Paul Custom, Ovation Legend acoustic/electric; 100-watt Marshall heads
- **Signature Song:** "Race with the Devil on Spanish Highway," from *Elegant Gypsy* (Columbia, 1977)
- **Classic Album:** *Splendido Hotel* (Columbia, 1979)

DANNY GATTON

I know a little bit of a lot of things, but I'm really not a master of any of them. —Danny Gatton

Fluent in jazz, country, blues, bluegrass, rockabilly, soul and rock and roll, Danny Gatton was a virtual encyclopedia of American guitar styles. "I always figured I could play it all," Gatton once commented. In live performance, he'd unleash barrages of blazing, melodic licks from his Telecaster, emulating organs and horn sections, whipping out lightning-fast banjo rolls and simultaneously playing walking bass lines while plucking complicated melodies. His mastery of a melting pot of musical styles made him a cult favorite among guitar enthusiasts, who fervently sought his records and flocked to his live shows.

Gatton borrowed generously from classic heavyweights like Les Paul, Scotty Moore, James Burton, Hank Garland and Charlie Christian, as well as contemporaries Roy Buchanan and Lenny Breau, combining those influences into a style that was truly one-of-a-kind. His suicide at the age of 49 on October 4, 1994, left a gap in the guitar community that may never be filled in our lifetime.

- **Equipment:** 1953 Fender Telecaster and Fender Danny Gatton Signature Telecaster; late-Fifties Fender Twin
- **Signature Song:** "Love My Baby," from Robert Gordon and Danny Gatton—*The Humbler* (NRG, 1996)
- **Classic Album:** Danny Gatton—*88 Elmira Street* (Elektra, 1991)

ALLAN HOLDSWORTH

He's out there, spacy and so into playing weird, but I love the sound he gets. He's probably the only guitarist who has made me go, "Huh? How did he do that?"

—Eddie Van Halen

A true artist who is more concerned with perfecting his craft than selling records, Allan Holdsworth has spent his entire career striving to push the guitar beyond its boundaries. Attempting to imitate the sound of a saxophone, he pioneered a fluid legato style that has inspired many jazz and rock guitarists, most notably Eddie Van Halen. Holdsworth's playing is characterized by unorthodox chord voicings, seemingly impossible fretboard stretches, unusual, dissonant lines, blinding speed and a smooth, swelling attack.

Holdsworth initially came to prominence playing in progressive rock bands, among them Gong, Soft Machine and U.K., but he has worked as a solo artist since the Eighties. He is one of the few guitarists to embrace guitar synthesis, and his solo album, *Atavachron*, remains one of the finest showcases of the instrument's capabilities.

- **Equipment:** Ibanez and Carvin signature models, SynthAxe; Mesa/Boogie Dual Rectifier and .50 Caliber
- **Signature Song:** "Metal Fatigue," from Allan Holdsworth—*Metal Fatigue* (Enigma, 1985)
- **Classic Album:** Allan Holdsworth—*Metal Fatigue*

ERIC JOHNSON

Guitar seems to be evolving into this new, great place, but I don't know if I like that fork in the road. I'm looking for the other fork in the road.

—Eric Johnson

One of rock guitar's most exacting perfectionists, Eric Johnson has gained notoriety for his flawless technique, rich tone and soaring melodies. Despite playing on several successful albums by artists such as Christopher Cross and Carole King during the early Eighties, Johnson was largely unknown until he released his second solo album, *Ah Via Musicom,* featuring the hit single "Cliffs of Dover," in 1990.

Johnson's violin-like tone and impossibly fast-but-precise string-skipping runs have made him one of today's most esteemed and imitated guitarists, while his tasteful melodic sense has helped him establish a mainstream audience. Equally at home playing jazz, country and acoustic fingerstyle, the versatile Johnson has an instantly identifiable sound and technique. His true specialties, however, are playing Hendrix-inspired rockers and majestic ballads. "I really want to find some way to make the guitar into an engine of inspiration that will last for another 20 or 30 years," he says.

- **Equipment:** Fender Stratocaster; Marshall 50- and 100-watt Super Lead heads, Dumble Odyssey and Overdrive Special heads, Fender Twin Reverb; Cry Baby wah, Echoplex, Fuzz Face, T.C. Electronic stereo chorus
- **Signature Song:** "Cliffs of Dover," from Eric Johnson—*Ah Via Musicom* (Capitol, 1990)
- **Classic Album:** Eric Johnson—*Ah Via Musicom*

YNGWIE MALMSTEEN

I know all the music theory there is to know. —Yngwie Malmsteen

Yngwie Malmsteen's 1984 debut, *Rising Force*, shook the rock guitar community and set a new standard for speed, grace and virtuosity. His "neo-classical" style, loosely based on the compositional structures of J.S. Bach and violinist Niccolo Paganini, was fresh and completely realized. By the time 1985's *Marching Out* was released, his influence was rivaled only by that of Edward Van Halen.

While the mighty Swede's star has faded in the U.S. due to the rise of alterna-rock, his contribution to the guitar must be acknowledged. Yngwie persuaded a generation of rock guitarists to look way beyond the blues box and explore such exotic fare as minor, diminished, harmonic minor and Phrygian scales.

- **Equipment:** Fender Yngwie Malmsteen Signature Stratocaster with DiMarzio pickups; Marshall 50-watt Mark II heads
- **Signature Song:** "Black Star," from Yngwie Malmsteen—*Rising Force* (Polygram, 1984)
- **Classic Album:** *The Yngwie Malmsteen Collection* (Polygram, 1992)

JOHN MCLAUGHLIN

Music is absolutely everything to me. It's given me everything. And so I in return have to give everything I have to it.

—John McLaughlin

As a member of Miles Davis' band and Tony Williams' Lifetime in the late Sixties, John McLaughlin was one of the progenitors of fusion. Abandoning the warm hollowbody tone and cool, laid-back attitude that had previously defined most jazz guitar playing, McLaughlin brought a wild, rock-inspired intensity to the music with his bright, distorted tone, almost reckless pursuit of speed on the fretboard and wild, overextended note bending that had more in common with blues screamers like Buddy Guy than any traditional jazz cats. His early-Seventies recordings with the Mahavishnu Orchestra were trailblazing adventures that forever broke down the barriers between rock and jazz while exploring Indian-inspired motifs.

Throughout the Eighties, he abandoned the electric guitar and devoted his time to expanding the range of the acoustic. His 1986 effort, *The Promise*, displays the breadth of his talents from traditional jazz and acoustic world music to heavy rock fusion and guitar synth-driven jungle music.

- **Equipment:** Rex Bogue double-neck electric, custom-made Abe Wechter acoustic
- **Signature Song:** "Reincarnation," from John McLaughlin—*Qué Alegría* (Verve, 1991)
- **Classic Album:** Mahavishnu Orchestra—*Inner Mounting Flame* (Columbia, 1971)

STEVE MORSE

All I want is the integrity of John McLaughlin, the chops of Eddie Van Halen and the musical finesse of Segovia.

—Steve Morse

Steve Morse's hands, it is believed, are permanently fused to his guitar. According to legend, he once kept his chops up by playing a small travel guitar as he drove around in his car, using his knees to steer the vehicle. Morse's storied devotion to his instrument, not to mention his awesome technical prowess, positioned him at the forefront of the second generation of fusion guitarists in the late Seventies. His band, the Dixie Dregs, played a unique brand of jazz-fusion that incorporated such disparate styles as Baroque classical music, bluegrass and hard rock boogie, giving the genre a Southern-rock spin that made the whole thing sound like the Mahavishnu Orchestra colliding with Molly Hatchet.

Morse's diverse playing style shifts focus in dizzying fashion, jumping from swift, precisely picked passages that span the entire fretboard to tight chicken pickin' and pedal steel-inspired bends. He makes effective use of odd-meter time signatures and key changes ("Ice Cakes," "What If") and lush, overlapping lines generated with a digital delay ("Night Meets Light").

Morse, who set out on a solo career in the Eighties, has been a member of the rock groups Kansas and, most recently, Deep Purple.

- **Equipment:** Ernie Ball/Music Man Steve Morse Signature guitar; Ampeg V4
- **Signature Song:** "Cruise Control," from Dixie Dregs—*Divided We Stand: Best of the Dixie Dregs* (Arista, 1989)
- **Classic Album:** Steve Morse—*The Introduction* (Elektra, 1984)

ULI JON ROTH

Uli Roth had the whole thing down: his technique, his tone, the Hendrixisms mixed with that Euro-classic style of modal playing. I think he influenced a lot more people than he's given credit for.

—Kirk Hammett

Whereas most heavy metal guitarists during the Seventies played cranked-up blues licks, Uli Jon Roth took metal into unexplored territory with fluent, Eastern-sounding Phrygian mode excursions, fluid and lyrical Hendrix-cum-Curtis Mayfield chordal rhythms and incredibly fast and precise melodic runs.

Inspired by Hendrix and Blackmore, Roth shared his mentors' attraction to dramatic tremolo bar work and thick, distorted Stratocaster tones. His work with the Scorpions helped set the foundation for the emergence in the Eighties of such classically influenced northern European guitarists as Yngwie Malmsteen, Adrian Vandenberg and

John Norum. Roth left the Scorpions in the late Seventies, just before the band achieved chart-topping success in the U.S. Since then, he has released a steady stream of Hendrix-esque solo albums.

- **Equipment:** Fender Stratocaster; 100-watt Marshall
- **Signature Song:** "Sails of Charon," from Scorpions—*Taken By Force* (RCA, 1978)
- **Classic Album:** Scorpions—*Virgin Killers* (RCA, 1976)

STEVE VAI

Steve Vai is a huge musician. Most people hear him as a guitar player. They don't see all the different pairs of pants he owns. But I've seen the pants and I've heard the tapes.

—Joe Satriani

Steve Vai just might be the most naturally gifted musician to ever play rock guitar. His unworldly chops once caused a fellow guitarist to speculate whether "he had an extra muscle in his hand."

The phenomenally talented Vai made his recording debut as a teenager in the highly challenging environment of Frank Zappa's band. He subsequently developed a reputation as the world's greatest hired gun, thanks to highly visible stints with David Lee Roth and Whitesnake.

Vai's awe-inspiring fretwork incorporates polyrhythms, unusual Dorian mode and whole-tone scales and humorous, bombastic melodies. Few guitarists have explored the possibilities of effects processors and the tremolo bar as extensively as Vai, who uses them to create a wide variety of sounds ranging from animal growls to abrasive warbles. His playing is far removed from the standard blues-based pentatonic licks that most rock guitarists rely upon, yet it maintains an attitude that rivals the heaviest metal music.

His 1990 solo album, *Passion and Warfare,* remains one of the high-water marks in instrumental guitar music history.

- **Equipment:** Ibanez JEM-777, Ibanez UV-7 Universe 7-string; Marshall 100-watt heads; Eventide H3000S Harmonizer, Vox wah.
- **Signature Song:** "Blue Powder," from Steve Vai—*Passion and Warfare* (Relativity, 1990)
- **Classic Album:** Steve Vai—*Passion and Warfare*

EDWARD VAN HALEN

Lots of people think a song without singing is not a song. Tell that to Beethoven and he'll kick your ass. —Edward Van Halen

The list of Edward Van Halen's accomplishments is long, vast and downright bodacious. Here's a partial list:

1) He revolutionized the way guitar is played. On the instrumental "Eruption" (*Van Halen*), Eddie managed, in the space of a mere minute and 42 seconds, to make two-handed tapping a must-have in every hard rock guitarist's bag of tricks.
2) He revolutionized guitar technology: with just $130 worth of spare parts, a soldering gun and some Schwinn bicycle paint, Eddie cobbled together a single pickup, Strat-style guitar that would serve as the template for virtually every guitar built in the Eighties.
3) He is an even better songwriter than he is a player.
4) He is the first and last guitarist since Jimi Hendrix who will always look cooler than you do onstage.

Ross Marino/Retna

Eddie Van Halen

5) He will also always have a better sound than you do: Employing nothing but a 100-watt Marshall Super Lead head, Edward Van Halen is responsible for the best damn tone ever to rock this earth.

- **Equipment:** Custom-made Strat-style solidbody, Ernie Ball/Music Man EVH, Peavey Wolfgang; Marshall 100-watt Super Lead, Peavey 5150 EVH; MXR Flanger, MXR Phase 90
- **Signature Song:** "Eruption," from Van Halen—*Van Halen* (Warner Bros., 1978)
- **Classic Album:** Van Halen—*Fair Warning* (Warner Bros., 1981)

JOE SATRIANI

As long as Joe's making music, I'll always find an inspiration to play.

—Steve Vai

One of rock music's most successful instrumentalists, Joe Satriani introduced the masses to virtuoso guitar in the late Eighties with his chart-topping *Surfing with the Alien*. The album demonstrated how a guitarist could fuse mind-boggling licks, a broad musical perspective and an incredible grasp of scales and music theory to memorable, tuneful songs—and earn a Gold record in the process.

"I'd rather someone said, 'Man, that's a great solo! I'll never forget it,' than, 'That guy's got some technique!'," says Satriani, who is no technical slouch himself. The guitarist burns his fretboards with intricate arpeggios, distinctive whammy bar screams and unorthodox scales, rarely wasting time with shopworn chord progressions or rock clichés.

A master guitarist and a master teacher, Satriani has seen former students like Steve Vai, Metallica's Kirk Hammett and Primus' Larry Lalonde attain an uncanny level of success.

- **Equipment:** Ibanez JS-6, Ibanez 540 Radius; various 100-watt Marshall heads, Roland JC-120; Scholz Rockman, Eventide H4000
- **Signature Song:** "Satch Boogie," from Joe Satriani—*Surfing with the Alien* (Relativity, 1987)
- **Classic Album:** Joe Satriani—*Surfing with the Alien*

Founding Fathers

CHET ATKINS

Merle Travis and I taught this country to play fingerstyle guitar, and I want credit for that sometime. —Chet Atkins

Chet Atkins was a guitarist and, as he might have said, a "music man" whose influence extends far beyond questions of genre to the way the instrument is made and played, and beyond that the way the music business works.

Atkins' distinct style of picking developed as an "upgrade" of the Merle Travis approach, involving the same sort of alternating finger-and-thumb picking but generally with three or four fingers in action rather than one or two. Atkins took an almost classical approach to his fingerpicking, carefully defining both the overall polyphonic texture and the counterpoint of individual lines.

The guitarist was an ubiquitous session player who signed with RCA in 1947 as a recording artist in his own right. In the mid Fifties, pulling double duty as an A&R man, the guitarist played an active role in RCA's signing of Elvis Presley, working as a rhythm guitarist and bandleader on such records as "Heartbreak Hotel." Atkins also played the acoustic "power chords" on Everly Brothers recordings, fashioning riffs that were later adapted to the electric guitar by Keith Richards, among others. His style of playing, both on electric and the nylon string acoustics he often favors, has influenced legendary players across the musical spectrum, from rockabilly Scotty Moore to Beatle George Harrison to jazzman Lenny Breau to just about every guitarist in country music. Chet Atkins passed away on June 30, 2001.

- **Equipment:** Gretsch Country Gentleman, Gibson Chet Atkins CEC; Fender Deluxe Reverb, Standel amplifier; Echoplex
- **Signature Song:** "Chinatown, My Chinatown," from Chet Atkins—*The RCA Years* (RCA, 1992)
- **Classic Album:** Chet Atkins—*Gallopin' Guitar* (Bear Family, 1993)

CHUCK BERRY

If you wanted to play rock and roll you would end up playing like Chuck, or what you learned from Chuck, because there isn't any other choice. He's really laid the law down. —Eric Clapton

Chuck Berry invented rock and roll guitar, but his playing was not without its influences and precursors. By far the most evident influences in Berry's playing, and the ones Berry himself always mentions, are T-Bone Walker and Carl Hogan, the tasteful, rhythmically incisive guitarist for Louis Jordan's Tympany Five, the most popular r&b group of the Forties. Walker, of course, strongly affected most of the guitarists of Berry's generation. It can be startling to hear fully formed Berry riffs, especially those ringing, hammered intros, showing up in T-Bone's recordings from the Forties and early Fifties, but they do.

However, none of the musicians who were Berry's inspirations really played rock and roll; Chuck did. He achieved a seamless integration of blues, country-and-western and pop. And of course, he wrote the songs that defined the first rock and roll generation: "Roll Over Beethoven," "School Day," "Rock and Roll Music" and others.

Berry put even his most blatantly "borrowed" bits into a strikingly fresh format, however. His pumping shuffle-rhythms on the guitar might be reminiscent of T-Bone's, but Berry's pianists had a much freer hand in embroidering around the rhythm, and on most of his classic records, the guitar shuffles are undergirded not by a rhythm-section shuffle but by bass and drums playing swing time—straight, walking 4/4. It's the tension between guitar shuffle and rhythm section-swing that give Berry's Chess recordings much of their get-up-and-go.

- **Equipment:** Gibson ES-350T, Gibson ES-355; Fender Dual Showman
- **Signature Song:** "Johnny B. Goode," from *The Great Twenty-Eight* (Chess, 1982)
- **Classic Album:** Chuck Berry—*The Chess Box* (Chess, 1988)

Holland/Retna

Chuck Berry

BIG BILL BROONZY

A good blues man don't play so much when he singing, because when you're moving them fingers too devilish fast, it takes away from your voice. The feeling all goes into your fingers. —Big Bill Broonzy

An early bridge between country blues and its urban cousin, Big Bill Broonzy also played a personal role in the development of British blues-based rock. Arriving in Chicago from his native Mississippi in 1920, he introduced a crisp, relatively intricate fingerpicking style that differed markedly from the work of most Delta-bred artists, reflecting pre-blues influences as well as a cosmopolitan familiarity with the many blue styles of the South and Southeast.

Broonzy was equally exceptional playing bouncy ragtime in C ("Skoodle Do Do"), straightforward blues in E ("Keys to the Highway") and flatpicking in open G ("How You Want It Done"). Blessed with an exceptional memory, he seems to have known a hundred songs, ranging from "folk blues" with an authentic pedigree to pop, ragtime and vaudeville-style "hokum."

Ever adaptable, Broonzy rapidly became the pre-war Blues King of Chicago, gracing literally hundreds of recordings on his own or backing other artists. But perhaps his most significant pioneering effort was yet to come. In the Fifties, having returned at least part-time to performing solo in order to cash in on the folk music revival, Broonzy made several visits to England. There he influenced the first wave of young British bluesmen, and he paved the way for Muddy Waters' first English tour in 1958. In August of that year, Broonzy died in Chicago; Muddy recorded one of his most impressive later albums in tribute.

- **Equipment:** Martin 00-28, Gibson Style O
- **Signature Song:** "See See Rider," from Big Bill Broonzy—*The Bill Broonzy Story* (Polygram, 1999)
- **Classic Album:** Bill Broonzy—*The Young Bill Broonzy* (Yazoo, 1991)

CHARLIE CHRISTIAN

Charlie Christian sounds old and brand-new at the same time. His solo on 'I Found a New Baby' is simple and complicated. It's as hip as any bop I've ever heard.
—Jim Hall

Charlie Christian was the first musician to realize the electric guitar's potential as a solo instrument in jazz. He improvised solos with the fluidity and power of a horn player, liberating the guitar from its traditional, exclusive role as a rhythm instrument and paving the way for the transition from swing to bop (not coincidentally, "Swing to Bop" was the title of one of his most famous recordings). Christian may well have heard the pioneering electric guitar solos of a fellow Texan, Eddie Durham, and he certainly listened to Lonnie Johnson and Django Reinhardt, both of whom played blazing single-string lines on acoustic guitars. In 1939 John Hammond, entrepreneur and A&R man deluxe, rescued Christian from obscurity and landed him a job with Benny Goodman's dance band, the most popular in the land.

While recording and touring with Goodman, Christian was based in New York City, where he took part in the seminal early-Forties jam sessions at Harlem night spots Minton's and Monroe's, credited with giving birth to bebop and the entire modern jazz movement. The content of Christian's improvisations became more harmonically sophisticated at this time, taking on the colorings of bop, though he remained a blues-rooted swing player with a special talent for designing riffs. His solos were generally melodic excursions—single-note lines with a floating, horn-like feel reminiscent of Christian's close associate, saxophonist Lester Young. Christian died of tuberculosis in his mid-twenties, but his relatively few recordings influenced almost every subsequent jazz guitarist.

- **Equipment:** Gibson ES-250; Gibson EH-150 amplifier
- **Signature Song:** "Rose Room" from Charlie Christian—*Solo Flight* (Topaz, 1995)
- **Classic Album:** Charlie Christian—*Solo Flight*

DICK DALE

The style of music I developed was the feeling I got when I was out there eating it on the waves.
—Dick Dale

As a child in Beirut, Lebanon, Dick Dale heard the sounds of Middle-Eastern stringed instruments, especially the lute-like sound. After his family moved to California, Dale was exposed to other sounds that stimulated his imagination: first the roar, pulsation and silvery harmonics of the ocean waves he encountered when engaged in his favorite pastime, surfing, then the roars of the lions and tigers he kept in a private menagerie. All these sounds can be clearly heard in his playing.

Dale's first gigs as a guitarist were in country bands, and he made several unsuccessful vocal recordings before he began steering his sound in a more danceable direction. His first hits followed in the early Sixties, instrumentals like "Miserlou" and "Let's Go Trippin' " that combined Middle-Eastern melodic flavor with the kinetic force of rock and roll. These records virtually defined the sound of surf music.

During his reign as the King of Surf Guitar, Dale also made the acquaintance of guitar designer and inventor Leo Fender. "My sound was getting real heavy and my amplifiers were not giving me what I needed," Dale recalls. "Leo started bringing me different amplifiers, and I blew up over 40 of them before he came up with the Dual Showman."

A lefty, Dale plays right-handed Strats flipped over and strung "backward" (with the low E string closest to the floor) with ultra-heavy strings, which help him get his huge, explosive sound.

- **Equipment:** Fender Stratocaster; Fender Dual Showman; Fender Reverb Unit
- **Signature Song:** "Miserlou" from *King of the Surf Guitar: The Best of Dick Dale* (Rhino, 1989)
- **Classic Album:** *King of the Surf Guitar: The Best of Dick Dale*

BO DIDDLEY

My music has a little bit of a spiritual taste, but it's also primitive. I play the guitar as if I was playing drums. —Bo Diddley

In the mid Fifties, Bo Diddley's slashing, instantly recognizable guitar rhythms put the "rock" in rock and roll. Drawing on the trance-like beats of archaic African-American "ring shouts" or "holy dances," he created "the Bo Diddley beat." Actually, it's more than a beat; it's a whole world of related, ultimately African-derived rhythmic accents, and it's influenced everything from rock and r&b to later developments such as funk and hip-hop. Bo also mined a fresh vein with his lyrics, borrowing from children's games, traditional contests of insults called the "dozens" and other elements of street-corner speech, style and humor. Some of his Fifties hits like "Say Man" layered spoken vocals over funky beats—rap records in all but name.

Though he was born in Mississippi, Bo, originally Ellias McDaniel, grew up in Chicago, where he acquired his nickname, of course, on the street. As a youngster, he studied the violin, and credits some of that instrument's standard playing techniques as an influence on his choked-string rhythm guitar playing. Bo also pioneered the use of controlled feedback, distortion and tremolo effects on his Fifties Chess label recordings. And from the first, he understood the visual as well as the aural appeal of the guitar. His onstage acrobatics were well matched by his eye-catching guitars, such as the series of rectangular custom-made Gretsches he's often seen playing.

- **Equipment:** Custom-made Gretsch electrics; Magnatone amplifier
- **Signature Song:** "Bo Diddley," from Bo Diddley—*The Chess Box* (Chess, 1990)
- **Classic Album:** Bo Diddley—*The Chess Box*

ROBERT JOHNSON

To me, he was just as great as Charlie Parker. The man did everything. He'd just sit down, tune a guitar, whatsoever you wanted him to play, he'd play it.

—Johnny Shines

Robert Johnson was a commercial also-ran during his own tragically brief lifetime, with only one minor blues "hit," the cleverly mixed sexual/automotive extended metaphor "Terraplane Blues." But beginning in the Sixties, when a new generation of blues-inspired rock guitarists began singing his praises and lifting his licks, Robert Johnson posthumously emerged as both a commercial and artistic frontrunner; his collected works have now outsold the records of any other country bluesman.

Admired for his complex fingerstyle/slide arrangements, Johnson baffled British Invasion guitar heroes like Keith Richards and Eric Clapton, who originally thought there must have been a second—and maybe a third—guitarist on his solo recordings. Almost as seductive as Johnson's playing is the harrowing supernatural myth—full of hoodoo hexes and a supposed deal with the devil—that surrounds his life. "Hello Satan, I believe it's time to go," he sang in "Me and the Devil Blues," and the assertion is still chillingly, utterly believable. Johnson eventually died from poison said to have been administered by a jealous husband; the singer-guitarist was only 27 years old.

Born in 1911 in southern Mississippi, Johnson grew up in the heart of the Delta, where the local musicians he listened to and emulated included Charlie Patton, Willie Brown and Son House. Beginning in 1936, the guitarist recorded the extraordinary body of work he is known for at a series of hotel-room sessions in Texas. His wounded-hound dog slide licks, percussive string snapping, driving "walking" patterns, intricate counterpoint bass lines, ostinato riffs and chording set the standards for blues guitar playing. His very ferocity and intense desperation have only become more appealing as time marches on.

- **Equipment:** Kalamazoo archtop, Gibson L-1
- **Signature Song:** "Crossroads," from Robert Johnson—*King of the Delta Blues Singers* (Legacy, 1994)
- **Classic Album:** Robert Johnson—*The Complete Recordings* (Legacy, 1990)

LES PAUL

My mother said, 'You've got to get your own style, play your way and be distinctive.' Yet, you've got to be commercial. I developed a style that changes to what the public wants. —Les Paul

Les Paul is both an innovative guitarist as well as a pioneer in the development of electric guitar and recording technology. Born Lester Polfus in 1915, he was first known as "Red Hot Red" or "Rhubarb Red" when he emerged as a more-than-proficient country-and-western guitarist. Playing live on the radio in the Thirties, he gravitated toward jazz, subsequently touring with all-star Jazz at the Philharmonic packages. His fresh-minded harmonies and bright pop sparkle have influenced everyone from Chet Atkins to Jimmy Page.

From 1949 to 1963, Paul's musical (and marital) partnership with singer Mary Ford yielded a string of catchy and sonically adventurous pop hits on which he regularly "stacked" vocal and guitar overdubs and manipulated tape speeds to great effect. Paul's recording experiments can fairly be credited with being the genesis of modern multitrack recording.

"Red Hot Red" also produced an early prototype for a solidbody electric guitar, which he presented to Gibson in 1940, only to have it rejected. By 1952, however, the company had changed its tune and were manufacturing their first solidbody electric, dubbed the Les Paul—one of the most popular electric guitars ever to roll off an assembly line.

- **Equipment:** Gibson Les Paul; Gibson EH-150 amplifier; custom-made Paulverizer effects unit
- **Signature Song:** "How High the Moon," from Les Paul—*The Legend and the Legacy* (Capitol, 1991)
- **Classic Album:** Les Paul—*The Legend and the Legacy*

DJANGO REINHARDT

Django Reinhardt was fantastic. He must have been playing all the time to be that good.
—Jimmy Page

Combining a strong European melodic sense with a love for American jazz and ragtime, Django Reinhardt executed lightning-fast chord substitutions, blazing arpeggios that scaled the entire fretboard and daring improvisational gambits and dazzling flourishes that greatly expanded notions of the guitar's capabilities in the early Thirties.

Born in a Gypsy caravan on the night of January 23, 1910, Django taught himself to play and was performing in Parisian dance halls and clubs before he turned 14. Already garnering a reputation as a genius, he made his recording debut accompanying popular accordionists in 1928. But disaster struck in November of that year when Django was badly burned in a fire that permanently crippled his left hand and disabled two of his fingers. Astonishingly, the guitarist gradually taught himself to play again, overcoming his physical limitations to become an even greater guitarist than he'd been previously. In 1932, Reinhardt began working with violinist Stephane Grappelli in the Quintet of the Hot Club of France, with whom he recorded his most influential sides.

By the late Thirties, Reinhardt was recording with visiting stars of the Duke Ellington orchestra, and after the second World War, he realized his lifelong ambition to tour the U.S. in the company of the Ellington Orchestra. Reinhardt suffered a fatal stroke in 1953 at the age of 43, but his brilliant recorded legacy ensures that he will not be forgotten.

- **Equipment:** Selmer modele Jazz
- **Signature Song:** "Nuages," from *Quintet of the Hot Club of France* (Musical Memories, 1992)
- **Classic Album:** *Django Reinhardt 1935-1936* (Koch, 1991)

ANDRES SEGOVIA

I think that the gift of music is a seed coming through generation to generation.
—Andres Segovia

Andres Segovia was certainly a genius, but hard work also played a part in his unparalleled achievements as a musician, composer and champion of the classical guitar. Segovia is said to have put in more than 100,000 hours of practice over the course of his life.

Born in 1893, the Spanish native did much to refine and develop stringed-instrument music over the course of his 94-year life. Among guitarists, Segovia is known for his varied tonal colorings, extensive vocabulary of expressive devices (portamento slides, etc.) and his florid, often controversial interpretations of certain baroque works. More than anyone else, Segovia is responsible for making the instrument welcome in classical circles. With his own transcriptions (from keyboard and orchestral scores) and revisions from the broader classical literature, and his commissioning new material from composers such as Villa-Lobos, he greatly increased the range of the repertoire available to classical guitarists.

Segovia also made significant contributions to the teaching of classical guitar with his books of scales and exercises, and through students such as John Williams and Julian Bream.

- **Equipment:** Fleta, Hauser, Ramirez classical guitars
- **Signature Song:** "Etude for Guitar #15 in D minor"
- **Classic Album:** *The Segovia Collection, Vol. 3. My Favorite Works* (MCA, 1987)

MERLE TRAVIS

Merle Travis has been the continuing influence in everything I've tried to do. I'd probably be looking at the rear end of a mule if it weren't for Merle.
—Chet Atkins

Known as a classic songwriter, singer and occasional actor in Hollywood westerns, Merle Travis will be forever celebrated among guitarists for creating and perfecting the picking style that bears his name: playing with the thumb and first finger in a quick, syncopated alternation.

Born in 1917 in Kentucky coal-mining country, Travis learned the style as a very young man, primarily from two otherwise obscure pickers Mose Rager and Ike Everly (the father of the Everly Brothers). In the Thirties, Travis gigged with various country string bands and worked with Grandpa Jones and the Delmore Brothers, whose performances were broadcast over Cincinnati radio station WLW. After World War II, the guitarist headed for the West Coast, where he became a popular attraction at dances, on live radio broadcasts, as a top-call session man and in various shoot-'em-up movies. In 1947, he collaborated with inventor Paul Bigsby on the design of what is considered the first modern solidbody electric guitar, as well as the Bigsby vibrato bar. The guitarist was active as a musician right up to his death in 1983.

- **Equipment:** Gibson Super 400, Bigsby solidbody, Martin D-28
- **Signature Song:** "Cannon Ball Stomp," from Merle Travis—*Walkin' the Strings* (Capitol, 1996)
- **Classic Album:** Merle Travis—*Walkin' the Strings*

Country Gentlemen

JIMMY BRYANT

Of all the guitarists I've known, Jimmy Bryant is the fastest and cleanest. He has more technique than any other guitar player that has ever lived. —Barney Kessel

Throughout the Fifties and well into the Sixties, Jimmy Bryant was country music's premier electric guitarist. Originally a fiddle player, Bryant learned to play jazz guitar from his army mate Tony Mottola and by listening to Django Reinhardt records. He eventually developed a style that combined fiddle licks with jazz sensibilities, giving country music an uptown appeal.

Working in Los Angeles recording studios, Bryant played on sessions for numerous country and pop artists, including Tennessee Ernie Ford, Tex Williams, the Ventures and the Monkees. But his most distinctive and influential recordings were his instrumental collaborations with pedal steel player Speedy West. Fiendishly innovative and bursting with chops, sophisticated melodies and blazingly fast solos, the duets have inspired many guitarists, including Albert Lee, James Burton, Dick Dale and Ritchie Blackmore.

Bryant was the first professional guitarist to play the Fender Broadcaster (soon to be renamed "Telecaster"), helping to pave the way for the acceptance of solidbody electric guitars. Sadly, Bryant languished in obscurity, playing in Nashville dives until his death in 1980, but his music remains timeless and immortal.

- **Equipment:** Fender Broadcaster, Fender Telecaster; various Fender amps
- **Signature Song:** "Stratosphere Boogie," from *Stratosphere Boogie: The Flaming Guitars of Speedy West and Jimmy Bryant* (Razor & Tie, 1995)
- **Classic Album:** *Stratosphere Boogie: The Flaming Guitars of Speedy West and Jimmy Bryant*

ALBERT LEE

Everyone rips Albert off, but nobody sounds like him. His phrasing is totally unique.
—Vince Gill

Albert Lee may be the most influential country guitarist of the last two decades. Lee's bright, percussive tone, ringing open-string licks and flowing chromatic lines resonate in the playing of every studio guitarist in Nashville.

Growing up in England in the company of players like Jimmy Page and Steve Howe, Lee started out playing blues-based rock. But the influence of James Burton and Jerry Reed led him to develop an intricate pick-and-fingers style, and he soon began playing country music.

"I gave an English rock edge to the country idiom," says Lee. After replacing his hero James Burton in Emmylou Harris' Hot Band, he recorded and toured with Eric Clapton and released numerous solo albums. Lee has played on countless sessions in Nashville, where he remains active.

- **Equipment:** Music Man Albert Lee model, Fender Telecaster; Music Man combos
- **Signature Song:** "Country Boy," from Albert Lee—*Hiding* (A&M, 1980)
- **Classic Album:** Albert Lee—*Gagged But Not Bound* (MCA, 1988)

BRENT MASON

The last thing you want to do is sound like a session guy on a session.
—Brent Mason

Pick up almost any country album recorded in Nashville during the Nineties and chances are that Brent Mason's guitar is on it. Fluent at everything from Albert Lee–style finger picking and Roy Nichols–style chicken picking to Grady Martin–style rockabilly flourishes, the versatile Mason has played on records by Alan Jackson, Brooks and Dunn, George Strait, Randy Travis, Trisha Yearwood and countless others.

While Mason is justly renowned for his incredible chops, it is his knack of coming up with memorable licks and the uncanny ability to sound like a member of a band instead of a studio musician that regularly gets him the best gigs in Music City.

- **Equipment:** Fender Telecaster; Fender Twin Reverb; various pedal and rack-mount effects
- **Signature Song:** "We Tell Ourselves," from Clint Black—*The Hard Way* (RCA, 1992)

CLARENCE WHITE

He's the first guy I heard who really knocked me out. He wrote a whole new book on bluegrass and electric guitar. —Jerry Garcia

As a member of the Kentucky Colonels in the early Sixties, Clarence White revolutionized acoustic bluegrass guitar with his rhythmically unorthodox approach to soloing and accompaniment. Playing electric guitar with the Byrds in the late Sixties and early Seventies, White made an even greater impact as a musician. His flowing rhythms, crisp solos and round tone on the groundbreaking *Sweetheart of the Rodeo* album helped break down the barriers between country and rock guitar.

A master at emulating the sounds of a pedal steel, White used a Telecaster equipped with a string bending device that he developed with drummer Gene Parsons (the device is now known as the Parsons-White string bender). Killed in a tragic accident in 1973, White remains influential among country, bluegrass and roots-rock musicians.

- **Equipment:** 1954 Fender Telecaster, Martin D-28 and D-18; Fender Dual Showman
- **Signature Song:** "Nashville West," from the Byrds—*Dr. Byrds & Mr. Hyde* (Columbia, 1969)
- **Classic Album:** The Byrds—*Untitled* (Columbia, 1970)

Jazzmen

LENNY BREAU

Lenny Breau has created a new concept and direction for the electric guitar.
—Johnny Smith

Even though Lenny Breau had deep roots in jazz, this master of the seven-string wasn't exactly a blues-based improviser in the traditional jazz guitar sense. A finger style innovator with an expressive range that stretched from Andres Segovia to Merle Travis, Breau had more in common with the tradition of George Van Eps and Johnny Smith—players whose mastery of harmony, alternate fingerings and sophisticated voicings transcend the instrument's technical hurdles and exploit its true orchestral potential.

Emerging in the Sixties as some sort of otherworldly musical miscegenation between Chet Atkins and Bill Evans, Breau possessed a keyboard-like command of chords, moving bass, counterpoint and textural devices that presaged the work of players such as Stanley Jordan, Phil deGruy and Charlie Hunter. The way Breau played was singular. He would juggle bass, melody and chordal devices in a fearlessly laid-back manner.

Breau's tragic death in 1984 deprived us of the opportunity to hear him evolve a more personal context for his expressive techniques, but at least we have one recording in print, with the prospect of more to come.

- **Equipment:** Holmes seven-string electric
- **Signature Song:** "If You Could See Me Now," *Lenny Breau with Dave Young*
- **Classic Album:** Lenny Breau—*Live at Bourbon St.* (Guitarchives, 1983)

FREDDIE GREEN

I don't know as many chords as Freddie Green. I'd be loaded if I knew that many. I'd probably go join a band and just play rhythm, 'cause he's not just playing chords, he's playing a lot of chords.

—Wes Montgomery

To a generation of players nurtured on the joys and dangers of single-note solos and overdriven electric guitars, the rhythm guitar stylings of Freddie Green might seem rather quaint. He never plugged in or took a solo, but you could set an atomic watch to his chomping beat. Originally a banjo player, Green hooked up with the Count Basie Orchestra at New York's Roseland Ballroom in the spring of 1937, and straight away Basie knew he'd found a rhythm mate. Along with drummer Jo Jones, bassist Walter Page and pianist Basie, Green was the rhythmic rudder on the greatest ship of swing ever to sail the seas of American music. Green remained as first mate for over 50 years, a constant on his big-bodied, high-action Stromberg archtop acoustic.

Green played infectious 4/4 grooves that cut through a wall of brass and reeds, carried the time and allowed Basie and Jones to engage in a coy game of cat and mouse—with each other and with the band's great soloists Lester Young, Herschel Evans and Buck Clayton.

Every time you go "One, two, three, four!" remember Freddie Green.

- **Equipment:** Stromberg Master 400, Epiphone Emperor
- **Signature Song:** "Topsy," with Count Basie
- **Classic Album:** Count Basie—*The Best of the Roulette Years* (Roulette, 1992)

JIM HALL

Jim Hall really pulled the guitar into the modern arena, moving beyond the music of the Forties and Fifties and stretching out into all sorts of ultra-modern harmonies, making really tasteful use of space and dissonance. It's hard to find a guitarist today who hasn't been moved by Jim Hall's sound.

—Tony Purrone

Of an entire generation of players who were initially inspired by the music of Charlie Christian, few managed to invoke the spirit of his art more while referring to the letter of his law less than Jim Hall. A master of tasteful, bluesy understatement and mellow, cello-like timbre, Hall seemed to grasp the lessons of Christian and Montgomery better than a whole skidaddle of players who might run rings around him in terms of knuckle-busting chops, but could never approach his gentle sense of humor or match his subtle feel for advanced harmony.

Following his formal studies at the Cleveland Institute, Hall relocated to Los Angeles, where he soon found himself a key member of drummer Chico Hamilton's trailblazing chamber jazz ensemble. It was there and in subsequent collaborations with innovators such as Paul Desmond, Bill Evans and Sonny Rollins that he became a hero to new generations of pickers for his ability to transcend the narrow parameters of guitar phrasing and entertain the fluidity and breathy cadences of the great horn players. Hall's rhythmic wit, melodic taste, adventurous harmonic command and blossoming legato touch have made him a spiritual beacon to this generation's most adventurous players, from Pat Metheny and John Abercrombie to John Scofield and Bill Frisell.

- **Equipment:** Gibson ES-175, D'Aquisto Avant Garde
- **Signature Song:** "John S."
- **Classic Album:** Jim Hall—*Live at Town Hall* (Musicmasters, 1990)

PAT METHENY

After I heard him, I had to admit he played pretty well; an incredible blend of Missouri, hip, chops—and all those teeth. —Gary Burton

Pat Metheny has been a major force in jazz guitar since he first exploded on the scene as the second guitarist (playing a Fender Electric XII) in one of vibraphonist Gary Burton's most visionary groups.

While Wes Montgomery and Jim Hall provided him with a formidable creative impetus, the angular compositions, asymmetrical lines, relentless rhythmic drive and deep blues feeling on maverick Texan alto saxophonist Ornette Coleman's *New York is Now* (Blue Note) really inspired Metheny to define his own direction. Metheny's playing is characterized by freely inflected chromatic passages, provocative use of space and rhythmic contrast, a dark, sweet attack (with just a hint of ambience), fluid legato shadings and horn-like intervallic leaps. Whether performing on acoustic guitar or guitar synthesizer, Metheny's lyric focus, rich harmonic pallet and rhythmic daring reveals a devout streak of post-modernism.

From his collaboration with Joni Mitchell to his radical solo guitar explorations on *Zero Tolerance for Silence* (DGC), Metheny has alternated between a variety of projects, but he always seems to circle back to modern jazz sooner or later.

- **Equipment:** Gibson ES-175, Ibanez signature model, Roland GR300 guitar synthesizer
- **Signature Song:** "Missouri Uncompromised," from Pat Metheny—*Bright Size Life* (ECM, 1976)
- **Classic Album:** Pat Metheny—*Song X* (Geffen, 1985)

Zsolt Fiscor/Retna

Pat Metheny

WES MONTGOMERY

I was constantly seeking verbal answers to the question, 'How do you do that?' The 'that' being improvising so melodically, for chorus after chorus, from single lines to octaves and finally to chords, and that gorgeous, warm, dark sound—all done with no pick, just with his unaided, unbelievable thumb. Wes' answer was always the same: 'I don't know. I just do it.'

—Steve Khan

Like everything else Wes Montgomery did, his innovative use of his thumb was purely intuitive—something that grew out of practical considerations more than anything else. When Montgomery practiced at home, the electric guitar's treble frequencies proved grating to his spouse. He tried all kinds of settings, but it wasn't until he put down the pick and used his thumb that she was mollified.

With a playing style characterized by octave unisons and an innate sense of melody, Montgomery honed his instincts for improvisation on thousands of rugged one-nighters and extended engagements in Indianapolis with his brothers Monk and Buddy. He toiled away in obscurity until Cannonball Adderley got him signed to Riverside Records. His pop-big band recordings with Creed Taylor and Don Sebesky made him a star, but just as the dues were paying off he succumbed to a heart attack.

No guitarist in the history of jazz was ever able to sustain a level of tension and release like Montgomery, and unlike many of his contemporaries, when he moved between single notes, octaves and chords, he never lost the emotional thrust or swinging continuity of his story. From Pat Martino and Pat Metheny to Stevie Ray Vaughan and Steve Vai, from George Benson to Jimi Hendrix and Eric Johnson, Montgomery's influence is ever-enduring and continually evolving.

- **Equipment:** Gibson L-5CES
- **Signature Song:** "S.O.S.," from Wes Montgomery—*Full House* (Live/AAD, 1987)
- **Classic Album:** Wes Montgomery—*The Complete Riverside Recordings* (Riverside, 1992)

JOHNNY SMITH

As far as I'm concerned, no one in the world plays better than Johnny Smith. They might play it differently but nobody plays better. Johnny could easily overplay, because he's got chops unlimited, but his musical taste would not allow him to make an overstatement. As a result, he makes delightful music.

—Barney Kessel

Johnny Smith's mid-Sixties Verve recordings were elevating and intimidating. Smith had conquered the instrument: perfect tone, an expressive array of subtle inflections and sweet, steely articulation.

For a generation of master players such as Pat Martino, Jack Wilkins and Larry Carlton, Smith represented the scholastic ying to Wes Montgomery's intuitive yang. "Moonlight in Vermont" was his breakthrough—a perfect illustration of his mastery of the guitar's subtle inner-string voicings and the template for every guitarist to come.

Even on his late-period recordings, it's difficult to believe that anyone could orchestrate such a perfect symmetry of line and chords with a pick, let alone get all the separate parts to glow with the dynamics one might more easily associate with classical guitarists such as John Williams and Michael Lorimer.

Smith's playing may occasionally come across as polite, but no one can deny the beauty of his line, the richness of his chords, the subtle underpinnings of his bass, the gentle precision of his swing and the tonal elegance of every note he's played.

- **Equipment:** Gibson Johnny Smith, Guild Johnny Smith
- **Signature Song:** "Jaguar," from the Johnny Smith Quintet—*Moonlight in Vermont* (Roulette, 1991)
- **Classic Album:** *Moonlight in Vermont*

Progressive Rockers

ROBERT FRIPP

I don't feel myself to be a jazz guitarist, a classical guitarist or a rock guitarist. I don't feel capable of playing in any of those idioms, which is why I felt it necessary to create, if you like, my own idiom.
—Robert Fripp

Studiously precise while simultaneously teetering on the brink of anarchy, King Crimson leader Robert Fripp's guitar playing is among the most distinctive in progressive rock. Fripp's ultra-disciplined cross-picking technique enables him to execute extremely difficult intervallic passages with remarkable ease and accuracy, as evidenced on Crimson's *Discipline* (1981) and his work with the League of Gentlemen. Fripp's sound also relies heavily on "Frippertronics," a tape loop system he developed that enables him to create lines with endless sustain.

Interestingly enough, some of Fripp's best playing came outside the confines of King Crimson: his solo on Brian Eno's "Baby's on Fire" (*Here Come the Warm Jets*), for example, is an exercise in inspired dementia. And you can't get more lyrical than Fripp's solos on the Roches' "Hammond Song" and David Bowie's "Heroes."

- **Equipment:** 1968 Gibson Les Paul Custom, Tokai Les Paul copy, Roland GR-300 guitar synthesizer; Roland JC-120 Jazz Chorus and Marshall amplifiers; two Electro-Harmonix 16-Second Digital Delays and a Roland Space Echo (for the "Frippertronics" system)
- **Signature Song:** "21st Century Schizoid Man," from King Crimson—*In the Court of the Crimson King* (Atlantic, 1969)
- **Classic Album:** King Crimson—*The Essential King Crimson: Frame By Frame* (Caroline, 1991)

DAVID GILMOUR

I've tried to approach my vibrato in the same way a classically trained singer does: you bend a note, hold it for a couple of seconds, then shake it.
—David Gilmour

Pink Floyd's David Gilmour is progressive rock's true master of space and time. While his lyrical soloing style is deceptively simple, his note selection and placement is flawless.

Gilmour's best solos, such as the breathtaking lead break on *Dark Side of the Moon*'s "Time," is so perfect it can stand as a brilliant composition on its own. On "Another Brick in the Wall (Pt.1)," from 1979's *The Wall*, he proves himself to be the undisputed dean of the compound bend (where an upward bend or release is resolved on two or more different notes). It's no wonder Gilmour's touch and uncanny way of squeezing maximum emotion out of every note prompted producer Bob Ezrin to comment, "You can give him a ukulele and he can make it sound like a Stradivarius."

Andrew Kent/Retna

David Gilmour

- **Equipment:** Fender Stratocaster; Hiwatt 100-watt heads, Fender Twin Reverbs
- **Signature Song:** "Comfortably Numb," from Pink Floyd—*The Wall* (Columbia, 1979)
- **Classic Album:** Pink Floyd—*Dark Side of the Moon* (Capitol, 1973)

STEVE HOWE

I never liked the 'in-vogue' guitar playing. I've always been a slightly traditional guitarist. Classical and jazz influences me a lot, but my music didn't come out the same, I'm glad to say. —Steve Howe

Steve Howe's eclecticism amazed, baffled and finally enlightened vast numbers of guitarists who were used to the "pentatonic box" soloing prevalent in the Seventies. Perhaps the most versatile guitarist of that time, Howe was adept at jazz, country and classical, from all of which he forged his own style.

His choice of guitars was also unique: his perennial fave is a Gibson ES-175, a hollowbody usually favored by beboppers.

In propelling the seminal progressive rock band Yes to the top of the charts, Howe introduced a new generation of guitarists to Travis picking ("The Clap"), harmonics ("Roundabout," "Close to the Edge"), classical guitar ("Mood for a Day") and modal and chromatic approaches to soloing ("Yours Is No Disgrace"). And lest you say he can't also rock, check out the Hendrix-inspired intro to "Siberian Khatru."

- **Equipment:** Gibson ES-175, Fender Telecaster, Martin 00-18; Fender Twin Reverb
- **Signature Song:** "Roundabout," from Yes—*Fragile* (Atlantic, 1971)
- **Classic Album:** Yes—*Close to the Edge* (Atlantic, 1972)

ALEX LIFESON

Soloing shouldn't be about how fast or how many notes you can play, or how much 'better' you can play than the next guy. It's got to really relate to the song or be a reflection of something in your character.

—Alex Lifeson

In the 27 years since Rush's debut album, Alex Lifeson evolved from being a heavy rocker in the classic Seventies power chord/pentatonic scale tradition to his role as rock's preeminent texturalist.

As Rush's compositional sophistication grew, so did Lifeson's guitar work—his favored use of suspended chords (played with plenty of chorus and delay) instead of triads defined the ethereal, instantly recognizable and often-imitated Rush sound.

Lifeson developed his signature sound by using arpeggios as harmonic pads underneath the vocals to counterbalance the band's driving, odd-metered riffs. Other Lifeson stylistic approaches include using notes on the top strings as common tones above a moving arpeggiated bass line ("Fly by Night"), incorporating open strings in arpeggiated sequences ("Closer to the Heart") and sustaining open strings over moving power chord shapes ("Jacob's Ladder").

- **Equipment:** Gibson ES-355, Gibson EDS-1275 double neck; Marshall and Hiwatt 50-watt heads; T.C. Electronic 2290 multi-effects unit, Roland Dimension D
- **Signature Song:** "Limelight," from Rush—*Moving Pictures* (Mercury, 1981)
- **Classic Album:** Rush—*Moving Pictures*

BRIAN MAY

I wanted to create a sort of violin effect that I could use to build orchestras from my guitar. That was a dream from childhood. I could hear it in my head.
—Brian May

Brian May's wall-of-guitars "wire choir" helped make Queen's 1973 debut a landmark event. His homemade "Red Special" guitar (built when he was 17), played through a Vox AC30 produced a singing, violin-like tone so mesmerizing and so unusual that the band felt compelled to place a "No synthesizers were used on this record" disclaimer on their album covers.

May would often overdub as many as 30 tracks to produce the symphonic guitar effect heard on cuts like "Keep Yourself Alive" and "Killer Queen." He was also the master of the Echoplex, as evidenced on "Brighton Rock"—live, he would piggyback two Echoplexes, play major and minor hexatonic motifs, loop them and then simultaneously play three-part harmony with himself, creating a cascading torrent of sequenced harmonized ideas.

Hardly a one-trick pony, May can play killer rhythm ("We Will Rock You") and authentically mimic rockabilly-style guitar ("Crazy Little Thing Called Love"). A true innovator.

- **Equipment:** Self-built "Red Special" guitar; Vox AC30 amplifier; Echoplex delays
- **Signature Song:** "Bohemian Rhapsody," from Queen—*A Night at the Opera* (Hollywood, 1975)
- **Classic Album:** Queen—*A Night at the Opera*

Rockabilly

JAMES BURTON

You don't walk onstage and play for other musicians. If you did, you'd starve to death. You play for the people.

—James Burton

The master of the memorable solo and driving rhythm, James Burton has played rockabilly, country and pop with distinction. He helped set the foundation for rock and roll guitar with his bright Telecaster tone, wild note bends, melodic double-stop runs and syncopated rhythms, and his "chicken-picked" lines remain a staple of country guitar to this day.

Burton got his start as a session player in 1955 at age 15 when he recorded numerous influential sides such as Dale Hawkins' "Susie-Q" and Bob Luman's "Red Hot." One year later he burst onto the national scene as a member of Ricky Nelson's band, frequently appearing with Nelson on the *Adventures of Ozzie and Harriet* television show and introducing millions of Americans to rock and roll guitar with his burning solos on singles like "Believe What You Say" and "Hello Mary Lou."

In the early Sixties, Burton laid the foundation for country music's highly influential "Bakersfield" sound by recording with artists such as Merle Haggard and Buck Owens. Later, he backed Elvis Presley and helped Emmylou Harris merge country and rock and roll as a member of Harris' Hot Band. Burton has worked with a variety of artists, including Frank Sinatra, Nat King Cole and Elvis Costello, and he remains an in-demand session player.

- **Equipment:** Late Sixties paisley finish Fender Telecaster; Fender Twin Reverb
- **Signature Song:** "Hello Mary Lou," from Rick Nelson—*Best of Rick Nelson* 1963-75 (MCA, 1990)
- **Classic Album:** James Burton and Ralph Mooney—*Corn Pickin' and Slick Slidin'* (Capitol, 1969)

CLIFF GALLUP

After hearing Cliff Gallup on the Gene Vincent and His Blue Caps *album, I was bitten by the bug. I remember sitting there being mesmerized by sounds I'd never heard before.* —Jeff Beck

Cliff Gallup was one of the most outstanding and innovative rockabilly guitarists. The solos that he recorded as a member of Gene Vincent and the Blue Caps fused the wild abandon of rock and roll with the sophistication of jazz. His playing on songs like "Be Bop a Lula" and "Cruisin' " was characterized by lightning-fast triplet pull-offs and diminished, major 7 and 6 add 9 chords, contrasting the blues-based solos and rhythms of most early rock and roll.

Heavily influenced by country and pop guitarists such as Chet Atkins and Les Paul, Gallup drew inspiration from various sources, including mainstream jazz and rock and roll, to develop an idiosyncratic style that showed that rockabilly music didn't have to be primitive and simple in order to rock. Although he recorded and toured with Gene Vincent for less than a year and recorded only 35 songs with the band, Gallup left an indelible impression on many guitarists, including Jeff Beck, Jimmy Page, Ritchie Blackmore and Albert Lee.

- **Equipment:** 1956 Gretsch Duo-Jet; Fender Twin, Standel combo with 15-inch speaker
- **Signature Song:** "Race with the Devil," from Gene Vincent—*The Capitol Collector's Series* (Capitol, 1990)
- **Classic Album:** Gene Vincent—*The Capitol Collector's Series*

SCOTTY MOORE

You've gotta hear Scotty Moore on Elvis Presley's Sun Sessions. He was truly amazing, and he was making it all up right there.

—Brian Setzer

In Memphis's Sun Studios in 1954, guitarist Scotty Moore, bassist Bill Black and hillbilly crooner Elvis Presley took chunks of Nashville country music, heaps of Mississippi blues and small doses of various other American musical styles such as bluegrass and Western swing and created rock and roll.

Moore's Travis-picked rhythms, bluesy leads and boogie runs became the blueprint of rock and roll for the millions of guitarists who followed in his footsteps, including Jeff Beck, Jimmy Page, George Harrison and John Fogerty. His playing shared the spotlight with Presley's vocals, establishing the electric guitar as the definitive rock and roll instrument as well as a symbol of youth and rebellion.

Moore recorded and toured with Presley throughout the Fifties until Elvis entered the Army in 1958. His energetic rhythms and melodically memorable leads graced the King's finest rockers, including "That's All Right," "Mystery Train," "Baby Let's Play House," "My Baby Left Me," "Heartbreak Hotel," "Hound Dog" and "Jailhouse Rock."

- **Equipment:** Gibson ES-295, Gibson Super 400; Butts Echo-Sonic amplifier
- **Signature Song:** "Mystery Train," from Elvis Presley—*The Complete Sun Sessions* (RCA, 1976)
- **Classic Album:** Elvis Presley—*The Complete Sun Sessions*

BRIAN SETZER

Brian Setzer is one of the foremost guitar players of the last half of this century. He's taken everything from jazz and blues to country and rock and roll and put it all together. —Reverend Horton Heat

In the early Eighties, when synth-dominated music ruled the airwaves, Brian Setzer and the Stray Cats spearheaded an unlikely rockabilly revival that rocketed the Long Island band to the top of the charts. Taking the music of Eddie Cochran, Gene Vincent and Buddy Holly and injecting it with a punk attitude and burning guitar solos that made even metalheads take notice, the Stray Cats resuscitated a genre that had been dormant since the late Fifties.

No mere revivalist, Setzer played with a sophistication and technique that rivaled that of the most esteemed rock guitar virtuosos. His solos are distinguished by fluent jazz chops, intricate fingerpicked arpeggios and runs, and raunchy double stops, while his rhythm work reveals his deep knowledge of chord melody.

Setzer is combining the swing sensibilities of big band music with the power of rock and roll in his current band, the Brian Setzer Orchestra.

- **Equipment:** Gretsch 6120; early Sixties Fender Bassman; Roland RE-301 Space Echo
- **Signature Song:** "Rock This Town," from Stray Cats—*Best of Stray Cats: Rock This Town* (EMI, 1990)
- **Classic Album:** Stray Cats—*Best of Stray Cats: Rock This Town* (EMI, 1990)

The Traditionalists

DICKEY BETTS

Playing music the way we approach it, there's gonna be good nights and bad nights and that's all there is to it. And what we do on a good night is something that you just cannot rehearse. Five days of playing means more than five years of rehearsing for us.

—Dickey Betts

Long overshadowed by Duane Allman, his legendary partner in the Allman Brothers Band, Dickey Betts always deserved the reputation for greatness he acquired only after Duane's 1971 death. Using elements of country, blues, Western swing and jazz, Betts fashioned a guitar style that is as beautifully melodic as it is rocking. His playing on the countrified "Blue Sky," the jazz-tinged "In Memory of Elizabeth Reed" and the joyous instrumental "Jessica" demonstrate his improvisational and compositional excellence.

- **Equipment:** 1957 Gibson Les Paul Goldtop, '54 Gibson Les Paul with Seymour Duncan pickups, Paul Reed Smith McCarty model, Gibson ES-335; Soldano SLO-100, Marshall 4 x 12 cabinets with 12-inch JBL speakers
- **Signature Song:** "Jessica," from the Allman Brothers Band—*Brothers and Sisters* (Polydor, 1973)
- **Classic Album:** The Allman Brothers Band—*At Fillmore East* (Polydor, 1971)

PETER BUCK

R.E.M. made a contract with the world that says: "We're going to be the best band in the world; you're going to be proud of us, but we have to do it our own way."
—Peter Buck

Peter Buck made it cool for punks to play clean. When R.E.M. emerged from Athens, Georgia, in the early Eighties, they brought with them a sound that would provide the perfect sonic solution for indie ears fatigued by the buzz-saw guitars of punk and the obnoxious keyboards of New Wave. Combining the chiming shimmer of the Byrds with the mysterious aura of early Pink Floyd and the speedy intensity of the Buzzcocks, R.E.M. were traditionalists who kept one eye steadfastly focused on the future.

Buck's relentless Rickenbacker-powered arpeggiations laid the bed for R.E.M.'s dreamscapes. He broke every chord into resonating single note bonanzas, weaving deceptively intricate picking patterns that put even the most well-trained right hand to the test. To top it all off, Buck plied his sound with inimitable style and pizzazz.

- **Equipment:** Rickenbackers; Vox AC30, Mesa/Boogie amps
- **Signature Song:** "Wolves, Lower," from R.E.M.—*Chronic Town* (IRS, 1982)
- **Classic Album:** R.E.M.—*Murmur* (IRS, 1983)

JOHN FOGERTY

A great rock and roll record has four elements: First and foremost, it has a great title. Number two, it has a great sound. Number three, it should have a great song. And number four, the best type of rock and roll record has a great guitar lick in it.
—John Fogerty

John Fogerty is rock guitar's living embodiment of the expression "less is more." As the dominant creative force in Creedence Clearwater Revival he ignored the various musical trends of the Sixties and early Seventies in favor of a hard-driving sound devoid of bombast and unnecessary adornment.

And Fogerty's guitar playing followed suit. Technically undemanding, clean and usually hummable, Fogerty's solos and rhythm parts on such hits as "Proud Mary," "Bad Moon Rising" and

"Fortunate Son" are understated—and utterly memorable. While Fogerty himself acknowledges his debt to some pretty earthy predecessors—Scotty Moore, Pop Staples and Carl Perkins, among others—his special genius is his ability to synthesize his influences into a very basic—and basically great—personal style. That style helped fuel Creedence's incredible collection of hits, at the same time teaching young guitarists that a solo doesn't have to be complicated to dazzle.

- **Equipment:** Rickenbacker 325; Kustom and Fender amps
- **Signature Song:** "Travelin' Band," from Creedence Clearwater Revival—*Chronicle* (Fantasy, 1976)
- **Classic Album:** Creedence Clearwater Revival—*Chronicle*

ROGER MCGUINN

The Byrds, to my mind, created one of the handful of original sounds in all of rock and roll history. Like Elvis Presley, the Who, Chuck Berry, and later Led Zeppelin or the Ramones, the Byrds created something that would influence most of the pop and rock that followed. —Tom Petty

If one band can be credited with inventing folk-rock and country-rock, it is the Byrds. Frontman Roger McGuinn, an accomplished banjoist and acoustic guitarist, came from a "traditional" background, having toured with folk groups such as the Limelighters and the Chad Mitchell Trio. But McGuinn was also influenced by Fifties rock and roll and the Beatles. In 1965, the Byrds recorded Bob Dylan's "Mr. Tambourine Man" and made history. With its 4/4 "Beatles" backbeat and McGuinn's arpeggiated 12-string electric guitar, the recording reshaped Sixties pop music by putting an American twist on the British Invasion sound. Although McGuinn also made important guitar contributions to psychedelic rock (particularly the spacy solo on "Eight Miles High") and with the help of Gram Parsons, to the development of country rock (on the landmark *Sweetheart of the Rodeo* [1968]), his early work remains his most influential. Among his disciples are Peter Buck, Tom Petty and a whole jingle-jangle generation of open-string strummers and pickers.

- **Equipment:** Rickenbacker 360 12-string electric, Martin 12-string acoustic
- **Signature Song:** "Eight Miles High," from the Byrds—*Fifth Dimension* (Columbia, 1966)
- **Classic Album:** The Byrds—*Mr. Tambourine Man* (Columbia, 1965)

RICHARD THOMPSON

I'm very influenced by pipe music and fiddle music. It's a singing thing. It's trying to create a voice on an instrument.

—Richard Thompson

If Chuck Berry had grown up in the English countryside and later spent some time hanging out with Django Reinhardt in Egypt, he may well have ended up sounding like Richard Thompson. Or maybe not.

Equally adept on acoustic and electric guitar, Thompson has always been a dedicated eclectic—from his early days as lead guitarist for Fairport Convention, the seminal British folk rock band of the Sixties, to his critically venerated recordings in the Seventies with his wife, Linda, to his solo work in the Eighties and Nineties. He has a fondness for Celtic melodies, but is just as likely to play a solo heavy with Cajun, Middle Eastern or bluegrass influence. His electric playing is characterized by a stinging tone (that he sometimes uses to evoke an exotic stringed instrument), hybrid-picked bending and a grim commitment to avoid blues-based clichés like they were the bubonic plague.

Thompson's propulsive acoustic playing is just as powerful and unpredictable as his electric work. One of today's truly great fingerstyle artists, he can re-create an Irish fiddle tune one moment and evoke an English music hall the next. A critics' darling, Thompson remains, unfortunately, the Unknown Soldier of Rock Guitar.

- **Equipment:** Custom-made Danny Ferrington electric, Fender Telecaster, Lowden L-32 acoustic; Fender amps
- **Signature Song:** "1952 Vincent Black Lightning," from Richard Thompson—*Rumor and Sigh* (Capitol, 1990)
- **Classic Album:** Richard and Linda Thompson—*Shoot Out the Lights* (Hannibal, 1982)

NEIL YOUNG

I just hate being labeled. I hate to be stuck in one thing. I just don't want to be anything for very long. I don't know why. I just want to keep moving, keep running, play my guitar. —Neil Young

He may be known to a younger generation as the "Godfather of Grunge," but Neil Young's influence reaches far beyond flannel work shirts and distorted power chords. He first established himself in the mid-to-late Sixties as a member of Buffalo Springfield, one of the more significant, if often overlooked, bands in the development of folk-rock and country-rock. After Springfield's breakup, Young

Richard Skidmore/Retna

Neil Young

simultaneously launched into a solo career and an on-again/off-again relationship with Crosby, Stills and Nash. He also formed a rock band, Crazy Horse, with whom he recorded such classic albums as *Everybody Knows This Is Nowhere* (1969) and *Rust Never Sleeps* (1979).

Young's guitar work with Crazy Horse is distinguished by grungy rhythm guitars and raw, unpredictable solos where scales are thrown out the window in favor of feedback, dissonance, improvised melodies, heavy vibrato and violent string bending. Young is also an accomplished acoustic guitarist, his unadorned playing heavily influenced by old-time country and bluegrass stylists. His acoustic albums, among them *Harvest* (1972) and its sequel, *Harvest Moon* (1992), are some of his most popular and critically acclaimed efforts. Although he's also dabbled in everything from blues and rockabilly to synth-pop, Young is at his best playing beautiful ballads and ragged rockers.

- **Equipment:** 1953 Les Paul with Firebird and Bigsby pickups, Martin D-45, Martin D-18, Martin D-28; 1959 Fender Deluxe
- **Signature Song:** "My My, Hey Hey (Into the Black)," from Neil Young and Crazy Horse—*Rust Never Sleeps* (Reprise, 1979)
- **Classic Album:** Neil Young and Crazy Horse—*Live Rust* (Reprise, 1979)

Space Cadets

SYD BARRETT

Syd's inventiveness was quite astounding. All those songs from that whole Pink Floyd phase were written in no more than six months. —Peter Jenner, early Pink Floyd manager

Rock's most celebrated loon, Syd Barrett managed to record a few precious albums and singles before he succumbed to insanity and disappeared from the public eye. His work with Pink Floyd during the Sixties included some of the finest examples of psychedelic rock, and he set standards of demented, over-the-top playing for the hordes of sonic psychos and axe murderers who followed in his path. Few guitarists to this day have been able to duplicate the orchestral cacophony that he generated with creative use of feedback, a wah-wah pedal and a slide. Barrett often seemed to be noodling aimlessly and anarchically when he played, but somehow his chaotic flourishes always ended up sounding charming and melodic. At his best, Barrett evoked hard rock, the blues, country, folk and experimental electronic music. At his worst, he would strum a single chord for an entire set, as he did in his final gigs with Pink Floyd.

Barrett was ousted from the band when his drug-induced ravings and bizarre behavior became impossible to control; later, his former bandmates helped him record two solo albums. Since then, this mad genius has been eerily silent.

- **Equipment:** Fender Stratocaster, Danelectro
- **Signature Song:** "Interstellar Overdrive," from Pink Floyd—*Piper at the Gates of Dawn* (Capitol, 1967)
- **Classic Album:** Pink Floyd—*Piper at the Gates of Dawn*

JERRY GARCIA

There are a lot of spaces and advances between the Carter Family, Buddy Holly and Ornette Coleman, a lot of universes, but Jerry Garcia filled them all without being a member of any school. —Bob Dylan

The transcendent image of a smiling Jerry Garcia onstage, playing for as long as five hours without repeating the same solo twice, remains forever etched in the consciousness of flocks of Deadheads worldwide. Garcia's playing encompassed virtually every genre of indigenous American music: bluegrass, blues, standards, jazz, country, jug band, folk, Fifties rock and r&b—a motley bundle tied together with his own stylistic ribbon.

Garcia was drawn to music by Fifties rockers like Chuck Berry and Eddie Cochran, but built his chops on acoustic guitar and banjo. In the Grateful Dead's early days, Garcia tended to spin out the usual Freddie and B.B. King licks, but eventually he matured as a guitarist, playing cleanly articulated, banjo-influenced lines on the electric

Michael Putland/Retna

Jerry Garcia

guitar in free-wheeling improvisations inspired by the bluegrass meltdowns of his early days.

"Since nobody was coming to see us, we had maximum freedom," Garcia said. "We could play anything we liked, and the idea of fixed arrangements went out the window." This lack of discipline could produce maddeningly meandering performances, but it was also central to the Dead's improvisational alchemy, which took listeners on multi-faceted journeys, with Garcia's slithering guitar serving as the vehicle. Garcia died in 1995, bringing the long, strange trip of the psychedelic era to a sad conclusion.

- **Equipment:** Guild Starfire, Travis Bean, Irwin Custom; Fender Twin Reverb
- **Signature Song:** "Dark Star," from Grateful Dead—*Live/Dead* (Warner Bros., 1970)
- **Classic Album:** Grateful Dead—*American Beauty* (Warner Bros., 1970)

ROBBY KRIEGER

When I first started playing electric guitar, everyone was playing Chuck Berry and B.B. King licks. I decided that I wasn't going to do that. I was going to find other avenues of expression. —Robby Krieger

Robby Krieger's dedication to finding his own path made him a singular voice in an extraordinary band, the Doors. Originally a flamenco guitarist, Krieger bought his first electric guitar just six months before forming the band. He quickly developed a distinct style that was perfectly suited to the band's experimental sound and unique lineup: a three-piece with keyboards but without a bass. "I really learned how to play electric guitar in the Doors," Krieger says. "My style was completely formed by the fact that we didn't have a bass player or a rhythm guitarist."

Drawing on his flamenco background, Krieger played exclusively with his fingers, allowing him to simultaneously cover bass, rhythm and lead guitar parts. His solos with the band were always well-crafted, informed by the same melodic sense that led him to compose rock classics like "Light My Fire," "Touch Me" and "Love Me Two Times." On 1967's "The End," Krieger utilized a dropped-D tuning and introduced Indian elements to his playing. Even his wildest excursions, like the demented slide lead on "Been Down So Long" or the two-guitar masterpiece of "When the Music's Over," remained eminently accessible.

- **Equipment:** Gibson SG; Fender Twin Reverb; Maestro Fuzz-tone
- **Signature Song:** "When the Music's Over," from the Doors—*Strange Days* (Elektra, 1967)
- **Classic Album:** The Doors—*The Doors* (Elektra, 1967)

CARLOS SANTANA

For pure spirituality and emotion, Carlos Santana is number one.

—Eric Clapton

It's hard to avoid words like "spiritual," "emotional" and "sensual" when discussing Carlos Santana, for it is the unassailable feel of everything he plays that makes him great. "Playing guitar is both a physical and metaphysical experience," says Santana. "My only goal is to always play from the heart."

Santana's heart has always found its beat in three distinct lifelines: the blues, percussion-heavy Afro-Caribbean music and jazz. From the day he formed the Santana Blues Band in San Francisco in 1967, Santana's music has been a unique fusion of these three forms, his playing charged with the soul and phrasing of blues and the freedom of jazz, and driven by fiery Latin rhythms.

To this day, Santana plays with a liquid-toned grace, subtly using dynamics to build a song's tension and playing at mach speeds without sacrificing a song's melody.

- **Equipment:** Gibson SG, Gibson Les Paul, Paul Reed Smith; Fender Twin Reverb, Mesa/Boogie Mark I combo
- **Signature Song:** "Sampa Pa Ti," from Santana—*Abraxas* (Columbia, 1970)
- **Classic Album:** Santana—*Santana* (Columbia, 1969)

Jacques Lowe/Retna

Carlos Santana

Free Radicals

THE EDGE

I don't feel that attached to my instruments. It's almost like I'm going to dominate them in some sort of way. I don't feel like they're part of me; they stand between me and something new.

—The Edge

Few players have done more than U2's the Edge (Dave Evans) to define the post-modern guitar style. The Edge showed how textures and rhythms, rather than riffs or chord progressions, could provide the main guitar interest in a song. A master of contrast, he often juxtaposed scratchy rhythms against ringing open chords that resonate with Celtic grandeur.

He exploited the Eighties avalanche of guitar effects to maximum artistic advantage, developing a signature style built on rhythms generated by a digital delay unit and creating a universe of soaring, echoing reverb timbres. Within U2, the Edge has always had free reign as principal colorist, with Adam Clayton's bass stating the songs' harmonic structures and Bono's sonorous voice providing a melodic center. The band's turn-of-the-decade shift from anthemic arena rock to jagged electronic rhythms and Nineties irony has given the Edge entirely new canvasses to paint.

- **Equipment:** Gibson Les Paul Customs, Fender Stratocasters, Gibson Explorer; Vox AC30 amplifiers, Randall combos; AMS digital delay, Roland SDE-3000, E-Bow
- **Signature Song:** "Pride (In the Name of Love)," from U2—*The Unforgettable Fire* (Island, 1984)
- **Classic Album:** U2—*The Joshua Tree* (Island, 1987)

THURSTON MOORE AND LEE RANALDO

We felt very liberated in the early Eighties because suddenly it was okay to be interested in anything—20th century composition, avant-garde jazz—rather than having to have that 'punk rules, everything else sucks' mentality. We were just interested in sound, and the mechanics of sound.

—Thurston Moore

Sonic Youth set the pattern for how an Eighties indie band could grow in popularity without losing credibility. Co-guitarists Thurston Moore and Lee Ranaldo combined punk rock attitude and song structure with open tuning techniques developed by downtown Manhattan avant-garde guitar composers Glenn Branca and Rys Chatham, and invented one of the most radical approaches to guitar in the history of rock.

A typical Sonic Youth song is a cacophonous affray in which guitars produce harmonic overtones and timbres that make Jimi Hendrix's version of "The Star Spangled Banner" sound as tame as "The Girl From Ipanema." Sonic Youth's guitar aesthetic has influenced several sub-genres of modern rock, from My Bloody Valentine's dissonant gloom pop to Dinosaur Jr.'s loud, minimalist indie rock and Seattle grunge. They reawakened interest in Fender Jaguars and Jazzmasters and motivated guitarists of every stripe to venture beyond standard tuning, profoundly affecting the sound of rock in the Nineties.

- **Equipment:** (Ranaldo) Fender Jaguars with a humbucker in the neck position; Pre-CBS Fender Super Reverb amp modified by Harry Kolbe; (Moore) Fender Jazzmasters; Marshall JCM 800, Peavey Roadmaster; ProCo Turbo Rat, MXR Distortion+
- **Signature Song:** "Kool Thing," from Sonic Youth—*Goo* (DGC, 1990)
- **Classic Album:** Sonic Youth—*Sister* (SST, 1987)

BOB MOULD

The early Hüsker Dü records remind me of just staring at your television when the cable goes out. All you see is snow, and all you hear is this big wash. —Bob Mould

Bob Mould is the Van Halen of American indie rock. Hailing from the same Minneapolis punk scene that spawned the Replacements and Soul Asylum, Mould virtually invented the alternative sound of the Eighties and Nineties the day he decided to drown Hüsker Dü's British Invasion-style pop melodies in buzz-saw fuzz and punk-fuelled angst.

But if Mould's grimy, first-position chording was as influential to the indie underworld as Edward Van Halen's two-handed tapping was to hard rock hopefuls, it was also as widely misunderstood and misinterpreted. Legions of hack imitators with little imagination and even less talent falsely assumed that an open G chord and a fuzz box were all you needed to get over. What they missed were the subtleties that make Mould's playing so enjoyable and worthy of examination: a mastery of voice leading, the knack for turning every open string to his advantage, a ferociously melodic lead style and above all, the uncanny ability to sound like two, and sometimes three guitarists at once.

- **Equipment:** Ibanez Rocket Roll Sr., Fender American Standard Strat Plus; Fender Concert, Yamaha G-100 head; MXR Distortion+, Roland SDE-1000 digital delay
- **Signature Song:** "Celebrated Summer," from Hüsker Dü—*New Day Rising* (SST, 1985)
- **Classic Album:** Sugar—*Beaster* (Ryko, 1993)

LOU REED

You can't beat two guitars, bass, drums. —Lou Reed

Lou Reed's restless quest to walk on the wild side of guitar playing is evident in his earliest work, the ultra-influential recordings by the Velvet Underground in the late Sixties. It's there in his droning "ostrich guitar" (where all strings are tuned to the same note), heard on "All Tomorrow's Parties." It's there in his gnarly, dual-guitar rave-ups with the Velvets' Sterling Morrison—a guitarist who so tastefully and sensitively supported Reed's own disquiet guitar probings that, to this very day, Reed still speaks with awe of that inexplicable, quasi-mystical "mesh" that two guitarists are capable of achieving.

Over the course of his solo career, Reed has toyed with all kinds of musical settings, from piano ballads to the proto-industrial noise guitar orgy of 1975's *Metal Machine Music*. But he seems to feel most at home in the classic rock band context: two guitars, bass and drums. He has recorded and performed with legendary axmen from Steve Howe to Robert Quine, but Reed has always held his own.

- **Equipment:** Pensa-Suhr, Fender Custom Shop Telecasters and Stratocasters; Soldano and Jim Kelly amps
- **Signature Song:** "Sweet Jane," from Lou Reed—*Rock 'n' Roll Animal* (RCA, 1974)
- **Classic Album:** The Velvet Underground—*White Light/White Heat* (Verve, 1967)

Sunshine/Hanekroot/Retna

Lou Reed

Visionaries & Madmen

BILLY GIBBONS

There's an old, famous phrase: 'This town ain't big enough for both of us.' With that in mind, it's either a six-gun or a six-string. If there ain't much more room in this town for both of us, then you'd better thrash.

—Billy Gibbons

With ZZ Top, his "li'l ol' band from Texas," Billy Gibbons stole the blues back from British rockers with a vengeance during the Seventies. Churning out a modernized, high-powered brand of boogie, the power trio shot the blues way past the Mississippi Delta and into outer space, centering their tunes around Gibbons' thick, lushly distorted Les Paul tones, harmonic squeals, driving three-chord riffs and tasteful-as-Texas-barbecue solos. According to Gibbons, the recipe for ZZ Top's success is simple: "Never add a fourth chord."

A consummate showman, Gibbons has appeared onstage with the strangest-looking instruments ever conceived, including velvet-plush-covered solidbodies and guitars with built-in television sets.

During the mid Eighties, Gibbons combined his nitro-fueled guitar playing with danceable drum machine beats and pulsing synth bass lines, beating like-minded industrial artists to the dance floor by several years. On their most recent album, *XXX*, ZZ Top returned to the band's blues-drenched past, and, in true Texas style, Gibbons' incredibly huge tone and fat distortion sounds bigger than ever.

- **Equipment:** Gibson Les Paul Standard, custom Fender Esquires and Dean electrics; Marshall 100-watt heads, various Fifties Fender tweed amps; Bisarktone ring modulator
- **Signature Song:** "Blue Jean Blues," from ZZ Top—*Fandango* (Warner Bros., 1975)
- **Classic Album:** ZZ Top—*Deguello* (Warner Bros., 1979)

SONNY SHARROCK

Imitating someone else's sound is unforgivable. No one remembers the imitators.

—Sonny Sharrock

A truly original player, Sonny Sharrock was an exponent of free-jazz guitar from the mid-Sixties until his death in 1994. Sharrock developed a jarring, avant-garde style inspired by horn players like John Coltrane and Ornette Coleman, and he eventually teamed up with Miles Davis, saxophonist Pharoah Sanders and other notable jazz artists for several monumental and daring recordings.

His jarring buzz-saw trills, fat-toned bottom string runs and shrill, above-the-fretboard slide work was often challenging and disturbing, yet chillingly beautiful. Sharrock often compared his work to a burning skyscraper or erupting volcano, an apt description for his glowing, yet dangerous musicianship.

- **Equipment:** Gibson ES-175, Gibson Les Paul Custom; Fender Twin Reverb, Marshall 100-watt 2203 head; ProCo Rat
- **Signature Song:** "Dick Dogs," from Sonny Sharrock—*Seize the Rainbow* (Enemy, 1987)
- **Classic Album:** Sonny Sharrock—*Into Another Light* (Axiom, 1996)

LINK WRAY

He is the king. If it hadn't been for Link Wray and 'Rumble,' I would have never picked up a guitar. —Pete Townshend

Enormously influential yet criminally overlooked, Link Wray is the prototype punk rocker and the original godfather of grunge. His crude distorted tone, primitive energy and do-it-yourself ethic inspired countless guitarists, including Pete Townshend, Neil Young, Dick Dale and Jeff Beck, and his influence extends from Sixties surf and British rock through Seventies punk and metal into Eighties thrash and hardcore to Nineties grunge.

Back in the Fifties, when most rock and roll guitarists were trying to avoid distortion, Wray was blowing up amps in a crazed pursuit of fuzz and sustain. In doing so, he conceived what became known as the power chord. Wray released dozens of outrageous instrumental singles during the Fifties and Sixties, including "Jack the Ripper," "Run Chicken Run," "Ace of Spades" and the coolest version of the *Batman* theme ever recorded, but "Rumble," released in 1958, remains his finest moment. Banned for being too suggestive, the instrumental shocked conservative America—without, it should be noted, the help of ghoulish makeup, explicit lyrics or onstage debauchery. Any young rebel who's ever donned an electric guitar, a leather jacket and an attitude follows in Wray's bootsteps.

- **Equipment:** 1953 Gibson Les Paul, early-Sixties Gibson SG; Premier amp, Fender Twin Reverb
- **Signature Song:** "Rumble," from *Rumble! The Best of Link Wray* (Rhino, 1993)
- **Classic Album:** *Rumble! The Best of Link Wray*

FRANK ZAPPA

I enjoy doing anything that is theoretically impossible and making it work.

—Frank Zappa

Frank Zappa may have written lyrics that were lewd enough to make a pimp blush, but his raunchy words pale in shock value compared to his outlandish guitar playing. Possessed of an unorthodox legato phrasing technique, horn-like distorted tone and a complex sense of rhythm, Zappa alternated among eloquently lyrical, melodic lines, harsh, jarring passages and mind-numbing flurries of notes, creating the effect of a symphony with a single instrument.

"I'm a composer, and my instrument is the guitar," Zappa told a British fanzine. "I shouldn't be rated as a guitarist. Rating guitarists is a stupid hobby." Although Zappa was highly critical of his own guitar playing, he released dozens of outstanding albums dominated almost entirely by his extended guitar solos, including the three-CD *Shut Up 'n Play Yer Guitar* collection and *Frank Zappa: Guitar.*

Zappa also surrounded himself with formidable talent and gave many outstanding guitarists, including Adrian Belew, Steve Vai and Mike Keneally, their first widespread exposure. A prolific composer, Zappa completed a huge body of outstanding work before his death in 1993.

- **Equipment:** Gibson SG, Fender Stratocaster, Performance Strat-style; Acoustic and Marshall 100-watt heads; Mu-Tron Bi-Phase.
- **Signature Song:** "Inca Roads," from Frank Zappa—*One Size Fits All* (Ryko, 1975)
- **Classic Album:** Frank Zappa—*Shut Up 'n Play Yer Guitar* (Ryko, 1981)

Punk & Disorderly

RON ASHETON

We practiced from midnight to six, just like that great Pretty Things song, 'Midnight to Six,' and then we made the record Raw Power. —Ron Asheton

In the annals of primitive six-string genius, few can compare to the Stooges' Ron Asheton, who used fuzz, wah-wah and distortion to create sonic poetry before he'd even mastered the technology. The evidence is there on 1969's *The Stooges* (Elektra), to many the ground zero of punk. His playing on songs like "Little Doll," "Not Right" and "I Wanna Be Your Dog," suggests that Asheton was learning his instrument as he went along (which he more or less was). That feeling of untutored discovery juices the music with an excitement that's still palpable more than a quarter of a century later. "C'mon, Ron—tell 'em how I feel," Iggy exhorts the guitarist during "No Fun," and Asheton answers him with a flailing solo that perfectly captures the sullen angst and inarticulate rage at the heart of the Stooges' music. The track fades out with Iggy praising Asheton's work: "Yeah—my man!" And a man for the ages.

- **Equipment:** Fender Stratocaster
- **Signature Song:** "I Wanna Be Your Dog," from the Stooges—*The Stooges* (Elektra, 1969)
- **Classic Album:** The Stooges—*The Stooges*

STEVE JONES

The Sex Pistols aren't into music. We're into chaos. —Steve Jones

Steve Jones developed his Chuck Berry-on-steroids style in amphetamine-fuelled practice marathons, where he fused the ham-fisted power of New York Dolls guitarist Johnny Thunders with the melodic savvy of Mick Ronson (Mott the Hoople, David Bowie). Jones' combination of brutality and melodicism did much to make the Sex Pistols' landmark debut, *Never Mind the Bollocks* (Virgin, 1977), so outstanding.

Cranking an early-Seventies Les Paul Custom through a Fender Twin, which he claimed he stole from the back of Bob Marley's equipment truck, Jones churned out power chords and ultra-tasty solos and fills, providing the perfect counterpoint to vocalist Johhny Rotten's venomous rants, anchoring the album in rock-solid guitar pop even at its most terrifying moments. Orchestrating constant tension between raw power and pop hooks, Jones revealed himself to be not only a highly skilled player but also one of the greatest guitar arrangers in the history of rock and roll.

And while many more guitarists have chosen to emulate Johnny Ramone's buzz-saw barre chording, this was primarily by default. Jones, an inimitable stylist whose command of the instrument defied the boundaries of punk, was simply out of their league.

- **Equipment:** Les Paul Custom; early Fender Twin with Gauss speakers, Marshalls
- **Signature Song:** "Anarchy in the U.K." from the Sex Pistols—*Never Mind the Bollocks, Here's the Sex Pistols* (Virgin, 1977)
- **Classic Album:** The Sex Pistols—*Never Mind the Bollocks, Here's the Sex Pistols*

JOHNNY RAMONE

I'm trying not to evolve too much. I always noticed with my favorite bands that once they evolved, they started turning into shit.

—Johnny Ramone

Like leather-jacketed Robin Hoods, the Ramones stole rock and roll back from the bloated, presumptuous supergroups of the Seventies and returned it to its rightful owners: obnoxious, snotty cretins. "When the Ramones started out, we refused to do any of that sissy hippie shit that was going on all around us," says Johnny Ramone. "The idea was to avoid all the overindulgence we saw in other bands to the extreme and to play pure rock and roll."

True to his word, Johnny Ramone's style couldn't have been any purer—or simpler. Playing a downstroke-only, barre-chord powered, no-nonsense approach that had all the subtlety of a well-liquored wrestling audience, Ramone and his low-slung Mosrite flipped the bird at guitar heroes everywhere. Two decades after the release of the Ramones' seminal debut album, his playing style still defines the sound of punk, hardcore and much "alternative" guitar—conclusively proving his theory that in some cases, evolution is overrated.

- **Equipment:** Mosrite Ventures II, Marshall amps
- **Signature Song:** "Blitzkrieg Bop," from the Ramones—*The Ramones* (Sire, 1976)
- **Classic Album:** The Ramones—*The Ramones*

JOHNNY THUNDERS

I feel a little dead tonight. —Johnny Thunders

If riffs could talk, every note that Johnny Thunders played would have snarled, "Fuck you." Raised on a steady diet of illicit substances, recycled Chuck Berry licks and rehashed Keith Richards riffs, the lead guitarist for the cross-dressing New York Dolls (and later the Heartbreakers) was the deadbeat dad of punk, sowing seeds of bad attitude everywhere he went. His bastard children, and a dysfunctional lot they are, include the Sex Pistols' Steve Jones and the Replacements' Paul Westerberg.

Thunders, who died of a heroin overdose in 1991, was an abysmally erratic player who veered from the marginally acceptable to the embarrassingly atrocious. Out of time, out of tune and always out of control, his solos were repetitive clichés, usually executed with all the indifference one might expect from someone who allegedly moistened his morning Wheaties with Jack Daniel's.

Perhaps the worst guitarist ever to become a legend, Thunders ruled because he was punk rock.

- **Equipment:** Gibson Les Paul Jr.; Marshall amps
- **Signature Song:** "Personality Crisis," from the New York Dolls—*The New York Dolls* (Polygram, 1973)
- **Classic Album:** The New York Dolls—*Rock 'n Roll* (Polygram, 1994)

Paul Slattery/Retna

Johnny Thunders

Unplugged Heroes

MICHAEL HEDGES

Nothing works if you try to be like someone else. Music is something you have to say yourself. —Michael Hedges

The release of Michael Hedges' debut album, *Breakfast in the Field,* 20 years ago, announced the arrival on the fingerpicking scene of a genuine iconoclast, a fabulous new voice among the herds of alternating thumb- and finger-specialists. Hedges discovered that far beyond the metronomic regularity of Travis picking and even the classical-derived counterpoint playing of the Anglo-traditionalists, there existed a brave, new acoustic world.

By banging and tapping on the face of his guitar and across the strings, Hedges created ghostly harmonic effects in compositions that rely on pure sound as much as melody for their effect. Hedges has been an idol smasher in other areas, as well: he has often played the harp guitar, an instrument long considered obsolete, and finds his musical heroes among modern composers like Béla Bartók.

None of this is to say, of course, that Hedges totally eschews melody, spits at Chet Atkins and laughs at traditional picking techniques. Even his "straight" playing is seriously spiced by his percussive patting, two-hand tapping and willful dissonances. Hedges, whose albums on Windham Hill are generally categorized as "New Age," has been, at least, a new wave guitarist who finds inspiration in unlikely sources and is unafraid to augment tradition with unusual inspiration.

- **Equipment:** Martin D-28, custom-made Takamine, 1920s Dyer harp guitar
- **Signature Song:** "Rickover's Dream," from Michael Hedges—*Aerial Boundaries* (Windham Hill, 1985)
- **Classic Album:** Michael Hedges—*Aerial Boundaries*

LEO KOTTKE

Playing guitar literally saved my skin. It gave me something to do for the rest of my life.

—Leo Kottke

Leo Kottke is the greatest exponent of what fellow fingerpicker John Fahey years ago dubbed "American Primitive Music." Blues, bluegrass, classical, pop—elements of these and other genres inform Kottke's guitar style, yet the sound he produces is peculiarly his own. More than 25 years after the release of his landmark debut, *6- & 12-String Guitar*, the album is probably cited by fingerstylists for having more impact on their playing than any other recording.

Kottke's sound is shaped by his facility with numerous tunings, banjo-style roll, thunderous picking—his thumb and fingers are like sensitive sledgehammers—and skillful left- and right-hand muting techniques that give his bass an unusual clipped effect. Delicate, melodic tunes like *6- & 12-String Guitar*'s "Ojo," perhaps Kottke's most perfectly realized work, soften the effect of his galloping arrangements.

In recent years, Kottke's playing has been more jazz-influenced than in the past. Also, he took the big step of removing his fingerpicks, resulting in a lighter sound with greater dynamic variance. Kottke remains acoustic's great power picker.

- **Equipment:** Taylor Signature 12-string, Bozo 12-string, Taylor 555
- **Signature Song:** "Ojo," from Leo Kottke—*6- & 12-String Guitar* (Takoma, 1970)
- **Classic Album:** Leo Kottke—*6- & 12-String Guitar*

JONI MITCHELL

My style is quite different. People were always telling me I was playing things wrong.

—Joni Mitchell

Joni Mitchell's syncopated rhythm playing and sophisticated fingerstyle technique shattered the stereotype of the singer/songwriter lazily strumming chords and picking simple arpeggios on a guitar.

"I think of the guitar as an orchestra," says Mitchell. "The top three strings are muted trumpets, the midrange is viola and my thumb plays a sparse, eccentric bass line. The thumb plays vertically while the rest of the fingers are swinging, which gives a funny kind of Senegalese quality to my shuffle, as if my thumb is playing a monkey chant and the rest of me is swinging like Robert Johnson on Mars."

Whereas most acoustic players employ a handful of open tunings, Mitchell has built her style around the use of more than 50 different alternate tunings, which she employs to play the unusual chord voicings that accompany her emotive vocals.

Michael Putland/Retna

Joni Mitchell

Ever since making her debut in 1968, Mitchell has sustained an adventurous and varied career. She found success as a "folk" artist, explored jazz-fusion with players like saxophonist Tom Scott, guitarists Pat Metheny and Robben Ford and bassists Jaco Pastorius and Charles Mingus, and dabbled with synth-oriented pop. Mitchell's influence is wide-reaching, inspiring guitarists from Jimmy Page and Slash to Prince and Richard Thompson.

- **Equipment:** Steve Klein custom acoustic, Martin D-28
- **Signature Song:** "Hejira" from Joni Mitchell—*Hejira* (Asylum, 1976)
- **Classic Album:** Joni Mitchell—*Hits* (Reprise, 1996)

JOHN RENBOURN

There's no limit to what you can do with the steel-string guitar.

—John Renbourn

Whether he's playing a ragtime tune, a medieval-tinged dance in DADGAD or a Celtic air, British fingerstylist John Renbourn does it with a touch and tone that sounds more classical than folk. But the well-schooled Renbourn (he actually teaches at a British university) is still the same musician who in the mid-Sixties played rhythm and blues with Hogsnort Rupert and his Famous Porkestra, an outfit that probably would have met with less than unqualified approval from Segovia.

But that is part of Renbourn's greatness—an ability to fingerpick on every side of the street, as it were. A big fan of Big Bill Broonzy, Renbourn altered his bluesy style considerably when he met up with British traditionalist Bert Jansch in the mid-Sixties. The two recorded some eclectic duo albums that ultimately led to the formation of Pentangle, the unique folk-rock ensemble, in which Renbourn played a lot of electric guitar. He later returned to the acoustic exclusively with his own traditional band. In recent years, he has recorded numerous lovely solo albums filled with his inspired originals as well as arrangements of everything from pre-Renaissance music to parlor guitar compositions—all played with the same elegant, "classical" approach.

- **Equipment:** Franklin OM, Guild D-55

- **Signature Song:** "Faro's Rag," from John Renbourn—*The Hermit* (Shanachie, 1991)
- **Classic Album:** John Renbourn—*The Black Balloon* (Shanachie, 1990)

ARTHEL "DOC" WATSON

I'd rather people remembered me as a decent human being than as a flashy guitar player.

—Doc Watson

A gifted singer, banjoist and guitarist, and a living repository of an enormous store of folk music, Arthel "Doc" Watson is a giant among acoustic musicians. His tasty, Merle Travis-inspired fingerstyle playing and fast, fluid and clean-as-a-whistle flatpicking—particularly his groundbreaking guitar arrangement of the fiddle tune "Black Mountain Rag"—demonstrated to a new generation of folk and country players that the days of the traditional boom-chick strummer were numbered.

In more than 30 years of recording, Watson has rarely recorded a solo without substance or a blazing fill without soul. His legion of protégés—Tony Rice, Dan Crary and Mark O'Connor among them—have been inspired by Watson's spectacular cross-picking and inventive accompaniments, but even more by his unflagging devotion to the instrument he rejuvenated decades ago.

- **Equipment:** Gallagher cutaway dreadnought, Martin D-28 with Henderson neck
- **Signature Song:** "Deep River Blues," from Doc Watson—*Doc Watson* (Vanguard, 1964)
- **Classic Album:** Doc Watson—*Doc Watson On Stage* (Vanguard, 1970)

The Three Funkateers

STEVE CROPPER

I get locked into a groove and defy everybody to tell me it's wrong. I want everybody to build around me.

—Steve Cropper

Perhaps the consummate r&b rhythm guitarist, Steve Cropper played with incredible taste and economy on many of the greatest hits ever recorded in Memphis' legendary Stax/Volt studios. His staccato chords and to-the-point fills propelled songs like Sam and Dave's "Soul Man," Wilson Pickett's "Midnight Hour" and Eddie Floyd's "Knock on Wood," while his work with his own band, Booker T. and the MG's, remains a model of inspired minimalism, especially his playing on "Green Onions."

- **Equipment:** Fender Esquire and Telecaster; Fender Harvard and Super amps.
- **Signature Song:** "Soul Man," from Sam and Dave—*The Best of Sam and Dave* (Atlantic, 1969)
- **Classic Album:** Booker T. and the MG's—*Best of Booker T. and the MG's* (Atlantic, 1968)

EDDIE HAZEL

In Detroit during the Seventies, there were a bunch of bands that were rock but funk, too. There were some serious guitarists in those bands, but they all wanted to be Eddie Hazel. —Randy Jacobs of Was (Not Was)

Dozens of guitarists revolved through the doors of George Clinton's various Parliament and Funkadelic lineups, but Eddie Hazel remains the most influential. His bluesy, psychedelic fretboard fireworks—particularly the extended solo on his signature tune, "Maggot Brain"—are often compared to Hendrix's work, but Hazel is distinguished by his innately funky rhythms and rocking, almost metallic riffs. Hazel's playing on Funkadelic's early-Seventies releases has influenced generations of guitarists, including Living Colour's Vernon Reid and the Red Hot Chili Peppers' John Frusciante. Hazel ripped it up onstage with Parliament-Funkadelic until he died of stomach cancer in 1992.

- **Equipment:** Fender Stratocaster, Kramer; Marshall 100-watt amplifier; Vox wah-wah
- **Signature Song:** "Maggot Brain" from Funkadelic—*Maggot Brain* (Westbound, 1971)
- **Classic Album:** Funkadelic—*Maggot Brain*

JIMMY NOLEN

Jimmy Nolen played simple grooves but he was tight, funky and relentless. He'd get you caught up in this hypnotic trance, and when he made a little variation in the pattern you'd go, "Whew!" —Nile Rodgers

Jimmy Nolen laid the foundations for funk guitar when he played his punchy E9 chord fills on "Papa's Got a Brand New Bag," the first record he ever made with James Brown. From 1965 until his death in 1983, Nolen recorded dozens of singles with Brown that featured his syncopated 16th-note strums, precise single-note patterns and timeless vamps.

Weaving chord patterns behind and around the horn arrangements that dominated many of the songs, Nolen drove the groove into listeners' brains, producing an effect that was more felt than heard. Samples of the guitarist's playing can be heard on many rap and hip-hop recordings.

- **Equipment:** Gibson ES-335, Acoustic Black Widow, Japanese Strat copy; Fender Twin Reverb
- **Signature Song:** "Let Yourself Go," from James Brown—*Star Time* (Polygram, 1991)
- **Classic Album:** James Brown—*Star Time*

TREY ANASTASIO

Music is like this portal into another world—the world of truth.

—Trey Anastasio

Trey Anastasio and his Phish bandmates picked up the tradition of psychedelic jam-oriented bands like the Grateful Dead and combined it with progressive rock to create their own potent brew. Despite protestations that he's not into playing solos, Anastasio is, in fact, a certified guitar hero, one who succeeds at getting arenas filled with teenagers to greet Mixolydian licks with screams of glee. In the process, he has turned a whole generation of listeners onto the ecstasy that is available to those who know how to play really well and to wail with focused purpose.

- **Equipment:** Languedoc custom hollowbody; Groove Tubes Dual 75 power amp
- **Signature Song:** "Billy Breathes," from Phish—*Billy Breathes* (Elektra, 1996)
- **Classic Album:** Phish—*A Live One* (Elektra, 1995)

Kelly Dervish/Retna

Trey Anastasio

What Makes a Great Guitarist?

A host of veteran players give their answers to this burning question.

CHET ATKINS

"Obviously, it takes a little talent and a hell of a lot of practice. Everyone has limitations, so one should work within them. It is fine to imitate, but eventually we must express our own voice. Also, listen to a lot to folks on the way up. I don't believe there are many times when I haven't learned something after watching great players and, sometimes, mediocre ones. To my way of thinking, there is not a great musician alive who hasn't practically slept with an instrument for years while learning. There are no short cuts! Learn the fretboard from stem to stern and practice scales for every known chord. Play for the love of it. Forget about monetary success and play what touches your heart. If financial success doesn't come, at least you have had a blast."

DICKEY BETTS

"I always thought that a great guitarist takes from the past masters and creates something all his own that can be recognized immediately. A great guitarist also listens as well as he plays, and isn't afraid to sit out or play something real simple and basic if that's what the song and the band call for."

JAMES BURTON

"A great guitarist is someone who plays commercially, is tasteful and very creative in having his own distinctive style. He also needs to have a great ability to communicate with other players."

DICK DALE

"You can create an endless rainbow of joy, happiness and total embracement with your fans, or you can destroy yourself, everything and everyone around you with your talent. Your music is an extension of your attitude."

THE EDGE

"The right pair of shoes, the right amount of attitude and an ear for what the singer is doing."

ROBERT FRIPP

"A great guitarist is true to the moment in which they find themselves."

MICHAEL HEDGES

"A good guitarist sees the original nature of the mind and channels it through the heart. The inspired guitarist adds some guts and makes you want to dance. A truly great guitarist forgets all this, and takes a chance."

ALLAN HOLDSWORTH

"It's not so much what makes a great guitarist as what makes a great musician, because a guitar is just an instrument, and an instrument is just a tool. A great musician is someone who sticks out like a sore thumb—in a great way."

ERIC JOHNSON

"A great guitarist is one who absorbs the implicit content and feeling of the special guitarist whom he or she admires. The guitarist then takes these building blocks and designs his or her own unique articulated voice from these players. A great guitarist knows that rhythm playing is just as important as soloing, slow soulful playing is just as necessary as fast virtuosic playing, and complete musical statements and compositions are the most interesting of these attributes."

STEVE JONES

"A big knob and dirty fingernails."

ROBBY KRIEGER

"All of my favorites have brought something new and different to their field. For every great guitarist there are 10 copies of him. They may be faster or technically better, but they can never have that original spark that he did."

TOM MORELLO

"Things like chops and innovations and feeling are important, but they don't in and of themselves make you a great guitarist. It's the ability to use them to communicate something and move people with your music. And, of course, it has nothing to do with popularity. I've seen guitarists in empty hotel bars in Moscow who blew me away."

BOB MOULD

"Instinct. A lot of people spend lots of time studying the instrument, but for me—having taught myself—it was all about instinct. And I think the same goes for players like Hendrix, Townshend and Thurston Moore as well."

CARLOS SANTANA

"You have to have the ability to touch the heart of the listener and inspire him or her to see and feel a positive spirit. A spirit that can help to heal this world."

PETE TOWNSHEND

"A great guitarist is never afraid to be different, find a unique approach, even a gimmick. A great guitarist is never afraid of spending time with better guitar players, and often seeks them out. There are a million reasons why this is a good thing.

"A great guitarist means tight trousers, good shoes, keeps strong fingernails, doesn't use chain saws, wears protection at all times (on Rollerblades). And a great guitar player invites God to every gig and has him sit on the headstock."

ANGUS YOUNG

"A well-tuned pair of shorts."

MALCOLM YOUNG

"Chuck Berry."

PART II:

The 100 Greatest Solos of All Time

To the rock guitarist, the solo is many things—the electric orgasm, the essence of all existence, the best way to impress sleek women. Not only do we love to play solos, we love to hear 'em. And the best solos thrill us beyond measure.

With that in mind, *Guitar World* asked its readers to compile a list of their five favorite guitar solos on a postcard and mail it in to our offices. The idea was that we would tabulate the responses and come up with a master list of the 100 greatest solos. Nice idea, huh? Well, you don't know the half of it. The cards came. And they kept coming. They came until we had to pack up and find offices big enough to accommodate the flood of cards bearing your well-reasoned votes for the greatest solos of all time. We counted until our arms ached, until we put together the list of solos, with some very cool commentary, presented over the following pages.

So, how did you vote? Ultimately, only one pattern emerged: The guitar heroes of yesterday remain the guitar heroes of today. And the great solos of rock's heyday in the Seventies are loved by the fans who heard them when they were new, and loved by the fans of today.

All this is as it should be, for we asked for the *greatest* solos. Greatness can be truly applied only to things that have withstood the test of time. As you'll soon see, *GW*'s readers intuitively understood this essential provision when they voted. The results scream for themselves.

1. "STAIRWAY TO HEAVEN"
Soloist: Jimmy Page

Album: Led Zeppelin–*Led Zeppelin IV* (Atlantic, 1971)

If Jimmy Page is the Steven Spielberg of guitarists, then "Stairway" is his *Close Encounters*. Built around a solid, uplifting theme—man's quest for salvation—the epic slowly gains momentum and rushes headlong to a shattering conclusion. The grand finale in this case is the song's thrill-a-second guitar solo.

Page remembers: "I'd been fooling around with the acoustic guitar and came up with several different sections which flowed together nicely. I soon realized that it could be the perfect vehicle for something I'd been wanting to do for a while: to compose something that would start quietly, have the drums come in the middle, and then build to a huge crescendo. I also knew that I wanted the piece to speed up, which is something musicians aren't supposed to do.

"So I had all the structure of it, and ran it by [*bassist*] John Paul Jones so he could get the idea of it—[*drummer*] John Bonham and [*singer*] Robert Plant had gone out for the night—and then on the following day we got into it with Bonham. You have to realize that, at first, there was a hell of a lot for everyone to remember on this one. But as we were sort of routining it, Robert started writing the lyrics, and much to his surprise, he wrote a huge percentage of it right there and then."

Plant recalls the experience: "I was sitting next to Page in front of a fire at our studio in Headley Grange. He had written this chord sequence and was playing it for me. I was holding a pencil and paper, when, suddenly, my hand was writing out the words: 'There's a lady who's sure, all that glitters is gold, and she's buying a stairway to heaven.' I just sat there and looked at the words and almost leaped out of my seat. Looking back, I suppose I sat down at the right moment."

While the spontaneous nature of Plant's anthemic lyrics came as a pleasant surprise, the best was yet to come. The beautifully constructed guitar solo that *Guitar World* readers rated the "best ever" was, believe it or not, improvised.

"I winged it," says Page with a touch of pride. "I had prepared the overall structure of the guitar parts, but not the actual notes. When it came time to record the solo I warmed up and recorded three of them. They were all quite different from each other. All three are still on the master tape, but the one we used was the best solo, I can tell you that.

"I thought 'Stairway' crystallized the essence of the band. It had everything there, and showed the band at its best. Every musician wants to do something that will hold up for a long time, and I guess we did that with 'Stairway.' "

2. "ERUPTION"
Soloist: Edward Van Halen

Album: Van Halen–*Van Halen* (Warner Bros., 1978)

It is hard to imagine a more appropriately titled piece of music than Edward Van Halen's solo guitar showcase, "Eruption." When the wildly innovative instrumental was released in 1978, it hit the rock guitar community like a hydrogen bomb. Two-handed tapping, gonzo whammy bar dips, artificial harmonics—with Van Halen's masterly application of these and other techniques, "Eruption" made every other six-stringer look like a third-stringer.

But the most remarkable thing, perhaps, about the unaccompanied solo is that it almost didn't make it on to Van Halen's debut album.

"The story behind 'Eruption' is strange," says Van Halen. "While we were recording the album, I showed up at the studio early one day and started to warm up because I had a gig on the weekend and I wanted to practice my solo-guitar spot. Our producer, Ted Templeman, happened to walk by and he asked, 'What's that? Let's put it on tape!'

"I played it two times for the record, and we kept the one that seemed to flow. Ted liked it, and everyone else agreed that we should throw it on the album. I didn't even play it right—there's a mistake at the top end of it. Whenever I hear it, I always think, Man, I could've played it better."

As for the distinctive echo effect on the track, Eddie recalls that he used a relatively obscure unit—a Univox echo chamber. "It had a miniature 8-track cassette in it, and the way it would adjust the rate of repeat was by the speed of the motor, not by tape heads. So, if you recorded something on tape, the faster you played the motor back, the faster it would repeat and vice versa. I liked some of the noises I got out of it, but its motor would always burn out.

"I like the way 'Eruption' sounds. I'd never heard a guitar sound like that before."

3. "FREE BIRD"
Soloists: Allen Collins, Gary Rossington

Album: *Lynyrd Skynyrd–pronounced leh-nerd skin-nerd* (MCA, 1973)

" 'Free Bird' was actually one of the first songs we ever wrote," says guitarist Gary Rossington. "Allen [*Collins*] had the chords for the pretty part in the beginning, two full years, but Ronnie [*Van Zant*] kept saying that because there were too many chords he couldn't find a melody for it. We were just beginning to write and he thought that he had to change with every chord change.

"Then one day we were at rehearsal and Allen started playing those chords, and Ronnie said, 'Those are pretty. Play them again.' Allen played it again, and Ronnie said, 'Okay, I got it.' And he wrote the lyrics in three or four minutes—the whole damned thing! He came up with a lot of stuff that way, and he never wrote anything down. His motto was, 'If you can't remember it, it's not worth remembering.'

"So we started playing it in clubs, but it was just the slow part. [*A demo of this version of the song appears on the Lynyrd Skynyrd box set (MCA, 1991)—GW Ed.*] Then Ronnie said, 'Why don't you do something at the end of that so I can take a break for a few minutes?' So I came up with those three chords at the end and Allen played over them, then I soloed and then he soloed...it all evolved out of a jam one night. So, we started playing it that way, but Ronnie kept saying, 'It's not long enough. Make it longer.' Because we were playing three or four sets a night, and he was looking to fill it up. Then one of our roadies told us we should check out this piano part that another roadie, Billy Powell, had come up with as an intro for the song. We did—and he went from being a roadie to a member right then."

On the studio version of the song, which appeared on Skynyrd's debut album, Collins played the entire solo himself on his Gibson Explorer, with Rossington playing rhythm on his Les Paul, "Bernice," and adding the slide fills on his SG. "The whole long jam was Allen Collins, himself," Rossington says. "He was bad. He was super bad! He was bad-to-the-bone bad. When we put the solo together, we liked the sound of the two guitars, and I could've gone out and played it with him. But the way he was doin' it, he was just so hot! He just did it once and did it again and it was done."

The resulting track was nine minutes long, and no one's idea of a classic radio song. "Everybody told us that we were crazy to put the song on our first album, because it was too long," recalls Rossington. "Our record company begged us not to include it. And when it first came out, they did all kinds of awful radio edits until it got big enough where it didn't matter anymore."

Shortly after the album was recorded, bassist Leon Wilkeson returned to the group after a brief hiatus and Ed King, his replacement, slid over to guitar, creating a three-guitar juggernaut that could

Scott Weiner/Retna

Members of Lynyrd Skynyrd

reproduce the song's majestic attack onstage. By the time Skynyrd cut the 1976 live album *One More from the Road*, Steve Gaines had replaced King and "Free Bird" had soared to over 13 minutes in length. This version, with its famous shouted intro, "What song is it that you want to hear?," triggered air guitar frenzy from coast to coast and firmly sealed "Free Bird's" status as a national treasure.

4. "COMFORTABLY NUMB"

Soloist: David Gilmour

Album: Pink Floyd–*The Wall* (Columbia, 1979)

How do you reason with two guys who once went to court over the artistic ownership of a big rubber pig? That was Bob Ezrin's mission when he agreed to co-produce Pink Floyd's *The Wall* with guitarist David Gilmour and bassist/vocalist Roger Waters. The legendary tensions between the two feuding Floyds came to a head during sessions for *The Wall* in 1979—which was why Ezrin was called in.

"My job was to mediate between two dominant personalities," recalls Ezrin. However, the producer turned out to be no mere referee, but contributed plenty ideas of his own. "I fought for the introduction of the orchestra on that record," says Ezrin. "This became a big issue on 'Comfortably Numb,' which Dave saw as a more bare-bones track. Roger sided with me. So the song became a true collaboration—it's David's music, Roger's lyric and my orchestral chart."

Gilmour's classic guitar solo was cut using a combination of the guitarist's Hiwatt amps and Yamaha rotating speaker cabinets, Ezrin recalls. But with Gilmour, he adds, equipment is secondary to touch: "You can give him a ukulele and he'll make it sound like a Stradivarius."

Which doesn't mean Gilmour didn't fiddle around in the studio when he laid down the song's unforgettable lead guitar part. "I banged out five or six solos," says Gilmour. "From there I just followed my usual procedure, which is to listen back to each solo and make a chart, noting which bits are good. Then, by following the chart, I create one great composite solo by whipping one fader up, then another fader, jumping from phrase to phrase until everything flows together. That's the way we did it on 'Comfortably Numb.' "

5. "ALL ALONG THE WATCHTOWER"
Soloist: Jimi Hendrix

Album: The Jimi Hendrix Experience–*Electric Ladyland* (Experience Hendrix/MCA, 1968)

Joining the Experience for the initial "Watchtower" session was Traffic guitarist Dave Mason, who, it was decided, would contribute a 12-string acoustic part. "Dave hung out a lot with Jimi and was a regular in the studio," says engineer Eddie Kramer. "Jimi was aware of his ability and felt that he could cover the part adequately."

Jimi, says Kramer, had a firm understanding of just how the song was to be arranged and performed, but the session proved to be anything but smooth. Mason, whose job it was to double Jimi's six-string acoustic rhythm part, struggled mightily, causing Jimi to reprimand him several times.

Hendrix and Noel Redding also clashed, and the bassist, angered by what he saw as Jimi's obsessive quest for perfection, bolted from the studio midway through the session. Mason took over the bass in Redding's absence, but Hendrix ultimately overdubbed the part himself, using a small, custom bass guitar that Bill Wyman had given to Andy Johns.

After the basic rhythm tracks were finally completed to Jimi's satisfaction, he turned his attention to the song's four distinct solo sections, each of which were recorded separately. "Once Jimi started working on his solos, the session moved very quickly," says Kramer. "The thing that occurs to me was how completely prepared he was. One thing that people don't realize is that Jimi always did his homework. He and producer Chas Chandler always got together to work out ideas well before he walked into the studio. Jimi knew exactly what he wanted to play

"He used a different tone setting for each part. I recall him using a cigarette lighter to play the slide section, and that the delay effect on each of the sections was applied later. I used an EMT plate reverb—that was the only thing available to us at the time."

6. "NOVEMBER RAIN"
Soloist: Slash

Album: Guns N' Roses–*Use Your Illusion I* (Geffen, 1991)

Long before the world embraced Guns N' Roses as the quintessential Eighties rock band, the L.A.-based outfit recorded in one day a demo tape that featured many of what would become the band's best-known songs, including "Welcome to the Jungle," "Paradise City" and "Mr. Browstone," all of which would wind up on the band's 1987 breakthrough album, *Appetite for Destruction*. Also on the tape was a song called "November Rain," a sprawling, grandiose piano-driven ballad that would lie dormant for the remainder of the decade, eventually resurfacing in 1991 on the band's two-record set, *Use Your Illusion*.

"I think that demo session was the first time we played 'November Rain' together as a band," says Guns guitarist Slash. "We actually did it on piano and acoustic guitar. As far as the guitar solo, it was so natural from the first time I ever played it on the demo that I don't even know if I made any changes to it when we did the electric version on *Use Your Illusion*. I never even went back and listened to the old tapes. One of the best things about a melody for a guitar solo is when it comes to you the same way every time, and that was definitely the case with 'November Rain.' When it came time to do the record, I just went into the studio, played the solo through a Les Paul Standard and a Marshall [*2555, Jubilee head*] and said, 'I think that sounds right,' " he laughs. "It was as simple as that."

7. "ONE"
Soloist: Kirk Hammett

Album: Metallica–*...And Justice for All* (Elektra, 1988)

"I had a very clear idea of where I wanted to go with my guitar playing on *...And Justice for All*," recalls Kirk Hammett. "Unfortunately we didn't have enough time for me to fully execute my ideas.

"We worked on basic tracks for six or seven months, and then I only had eight or nine days to record all my leads because we were heading out on the Monsters of Rock tour [with Van Halen, Scorpions, Dokken and Kingdom Come]. To get that done, I had to do incredibly long, grueling days—like 20 hours at a pop—and it took so much out of me. As soon as I finished one solo, I had to do the next one. There was no time to breathe, as the whole vibe was to do it the best you could and keep moving. It was a pretty frustrating experience, to be honest."

Despite these frustrations, Hammett was immediately pleased with most of his work on "One," which featured three very different solos. "The first solo and the last solo were completely worked out in advance because I had been playing them for months," recalls Hammett. "So in those cases it was just a matter of fitting in tone-wise. I elected to use a clean sound in the intro solo, which was the first time we used that kind of sound. I dialed it up on an ADA preamp and, once we found the right sound, it just flowed. For the final solo, I used my conventional lead sound of the time. That one flowed quickly, too—once I worked out the intro right-hand tapping technique, a process I really enjoyed. I wanted a high-energy intro that would be different from anything I had done in the past. So I got those two solos done quickly and was pleased with them. But the middle one just wasn't happening."

Ultimately, Hammett was so displeased with the results of his second solo that he returned to the studio in the midst of the Monsters of Rock tour—spending a day at New York's Hit Factory with producer Ed Stasium. "I redid the entire second half of the second solo and worked to make it all fit in," Hammett recalls. "It was better, although I was never totally satisfied with it. I guess I did a good enough job."

Apparently so. The song would soon become Metallica's first legitimate radio and MTV hit, its solos firmly established as Hammett signature licks.

8. "HOTEL CALIFORNIA"
Soloists: Don Felder, Joe Walsh

Album: The Eagles–*Hotel California* (Asylum, 1976)

Credit for the guitar majesty of "Hotel California" is often given to Joe Walsh, who toughened up the Eagles' laid-back California sound when he joined the band just prior to the *Hotel California* album's recording. Actually, the primary guitar heard throughout the solo belongs to Don Felder, who wrote the music for the track and actually conceived and played the solo's intricate harmonies on his initial, instrumental demo.

"Every once in a while it seems like the cosmos part and something great plops into your lap," says Felder. "That's how it was with 'Hotel California.' I had just leased this beach house in Malibu and was sitting in the living room with all the doors wide open on a spectacular July day, probably in '75. I was soaking wet in a bathing suit, sitting on the couch, thinking the world is a wonderful place to be and tinkling around with this acoustic 12-string when those 'Hotel California' chords just oozed out. I had a TEAC four-track set up in a back bedroom, and I ran back there to put this idea down before I forgot it.

"I set this old rhythm ace to play a cha-cha beat, set the right tempo and played the 12-string on top of it. A few days later, I went back and listened to it and it sounded pretty unique, so I came up with a bass line. A few days after that, I added some electric guitars. Everything was mixed down to mono, ping-ponging back and forth on this little four-track. Finally, I wound up with a cassette that had virtually the entire arrangement that appeared on the record, verbatim, with the exception of a few Joe Walsh licks on the end. All the harmony guitar stuff was there, as was my solo.

"Then I gave it to Don Henley on a tape with eight or 10 ideas, and he came back and said, 'I really love the one that sounds like a Matador…like you're in Mexico.' We worked it all up and went into the studio and recorded it as I wrote it—in E minor, just regular, open chords in standard tuning—and made this killer track. All the electric guitars were big and fat and the 12-string was nice and full. Then Henley came back and said, 'It's in the wrong key.' So I said, 'What do you need? D? F sharp?'…hoping that we could varispeed the tape. But he said no, that wouldn't work, and we sat down and started trying to figure out the key—and it turned out to be B minor! So out comes the capo, way up on the seventh fret. We re-recorded the song in B minor and all of a sudden the guitar sounds really small and the whole track just shrinks! It was horrible, so we went back and tried it again. Luckily, we came up with a better version in B minor.

"I kept the capo on and recorded the acoustic guitar through a Leslie. They took a D.I. out of the console and a stereo Leslie, and they got this swirly effect. Then I went back and did most of the guitars, except for the stuff where Joe and I set up on two stools and ran the harmony parts down. I play the first solo, then it's Joe. Then we trade lines and then we go into the lead harmonies.

"Now that I've heard it for 20 years, the 12-string part sounds right to me, but it's still not as nice as the E minor version we did. And even when we'd finished the song and made it the title track, I wasn't convinced that it should be our single. I thought it was way too long—twice the normal radio length—and sort of weird because it started out quiet and had this quiet breakdown section in the middle. I was very skeptical, but I yielded to the wisdom of Henley."

9. "CRAZY TRAIN"
Soloist: Randy Rhoads

Album: Ozzy Osbourne–*Blizzard of Ozz* (Epic, 1981)

Guitarist Randy Rhoads employed a two-part process when recording his solos for *Blizzard of Ozz*, Ozzy Osbourne's first album following his ouster from Black Sabbath. First, the classically trained young shredder would take his customized Jackson guitars to a stone room downstairs at England's Ridge Farm Studios where he would work out each of his solos, among them "Crazy Train."

"This was after we did the backing tracks," says *Blizzard of Ozz* engineer Max Norman. "Randy had a Marshall and a couple of 4 x 12s, and we had him set up in this room with the cabinets facing up out into the main studio. They were miked at various points: close, at three feet and again at about 12 feet. I would make Randy a loop of the solo section and we'd just let that play into these big monitors downstairs, where he would just sit and jam away for hours and hours until he had composed his completed solo."

With the solos arranged to his liking, Rhoads would then report upstairs to the control room to record them.

"We'd plug the guitar directly into the console," recalls Norman. "We'd preamp it in the console and send it down to the amp from there. That way we could control the amount of gain that hit the amp, which is always a problem when running a remote amplifier and trying to get a good enough signal to it.

"Randy would put down his solos pretty quickly once he had them worked out. We'd do two or three takes to get the majority of the solo down, then maybe punch in a few little fix-ups. He'd try to get the first take as good as possible, then he'd double it and triple it. Ozzy always wondered why Randy double-tracked everything, and he really didn't want him to. I must admit, at the time I really didn't think it was a very good idea, either—but when you double- and triple-track a solo, it actually adds to the accuracy because it's somewhat more forgiving as far as pitch and timing; it blurs the edges.

"Of the three tracks on each solo, the one that we liked the best would be pretty much down the center of the mix, and the other two would be ghosted back three or four db, swung out pretty wide on either side. What happens then is that it doesn't become such an obvious double or triple track—it's more of an effect, really, because you tend to get the phasing between the different pitches. In addition, with guitars two and three panned left and right, you get a fourth guitar—a phantom guitar—in the middle. So what Randy's got on those solos is a double-track of his main guitar, and the other two guitars attempting to create a ghost guitar. It actually averages out pretty well—it works better than you might think."

10. "CROSSROADS"
Soloist: Eric Clapton

Album: Cream–*Wheels of Fire* (Polydor, 1968)

For more than three decades, Eric Clapton has been bemused by his fans' adulation of his solo on Cream's radical reworking of bluesman Robert Johnson's signature tune, "Crossroads."

"It's so funny, this," Clapton says. "I've always had that held up as like, 'This is one of the great landmarks of guitar playing.' But most of that solo is on the wrong beat. Instead of playing on the two and the four, I'm playing on the one and the three and thinking, That's the off beat. No wonder people think it's so good—because it's fucking wrong." [*laughs*]

Perhaps one reason for Clapton's difficulty finding the downbeat was that the concert at which the song was recorded, at San Francisco's Winterland Ballroom, got a late start due to drummer Ginger Baker's tardy, and rather dramatic, appearance. Recalls Tom Dowd, who engineered the recording and ran the mobile recording unit that night: "The group was supposed to go on and we didn't have Ginger and couldn't figure out where the heck he was. We were worried, and [promoter] Bill Graham and others said, 'God, I hope he's okay. Maybe we should call the police.' Then I look out from our vantage point upstairs and see a Corvette speeding toward us, with a couple of police cars a block behind it. That was Ginger arriving. I have no idea what happened, but he pulled up to the stage entrance, abandoned the car, ran up onstage and the band started playing."

And what they played is what you hear; contrary to a persistent, widely held rumor, the solo on "Crossroads" was not edited down.

"It's not edited and I've got an audience tape from the same show which verifies that," says Bill Levenson, who produced the Cream box set, *Those Were the Days* (Polydor). "That was a typical performance of the song. I've listened to a lot of tapes and all of the 'Crossroads' that I've heard come in at four minutes and change. They never seemed to expand it beyond that."

11. "VOODOO CHILD (SLIGHT RETURN)"
Soloist: Jimi Hendrix

Album: The Jimi Hendrix Experience–*Electric Ladyland* (Experience Hendrix/MCA, 1968)

Jimi Hendrix's publicist, Michael Goldstein, had successfully arranged for ABC-TV to produce a short news feature based primarily on the Experience's triumphant success in America. Filming began on May 3, 1968, with 16mm cameras capturing the recording of "Voodoo Child (Slight Return)," which, like many Hendrix songs, borrowed both musical and lyrical themes from Muddy Waters and other Delta bluesmen.

" 'Voodoo Child' was something Jimi brought in, and we learned that song right on the spot in front of the cameras," recalls bassist Noel Redding. "We ran through it about three times, and that was it."

It is not known whether ABC ever used any of the footage. And, unfortunately, all the camera originals were stolen from ABC's archives sometime after Jimi's death. The reel also included footage of the group performing at the Fillmore East and the Miami Pop Festival.

Engineer Eddie Kramer recalls: " 'Voodoo Child (Slight Return)' was recorded the day after Jimi tracked 'Voodoo Chile,' the extended jam on *Electric Ladyland* featuring Traffic's Stevie Winwood on organ and Jefferson Airplane bassist Jack Casady. Basically, Jimi used the same setup—his Strat through a nice, warm Fender Bassman amp. Jimi's sound on both tracks is remarkably consistent, leading some to think they were recorded at the same session."

12. "JOHNNY B. GOODE"

Soloist: Chuck Berry

Album: *His Best, Volume One* (MCA, 1997)

Chuck Berry helped shape rock and roll by mixing elements of blues and country, adding some boogie woogie piano, and kicking it all together with his own slashing shuffle rhythms. Berry also was instrumental in making the electric guitar rock and roll's primary instrument. In fact, for many years rock guitar was practically defined by Berry's distinct, T-Bone Walker-inspired doublestops and frequent, dramatic use of slides, slurs and bends. A renaissance man rocker, Berry was not only a brilliant guitarist and performer, but was unparalleled as a songwriter as well. And his most enduring song, appropriately, celebrated himself; "Johnny B. Goode" was a thinly disguised account of Berry's rise to international stardom.

"The song had its birth when a [*1955*] tour first brought me to New Orleans, a place I'd longed to visit ever since hearing Muddy Waters' lyrics, 'Going down to Louisiana way behind the sun,' " writes Berry in his autobiography. "That inspiration, combined with little bits of dad's stories and the thrill of seeing my black name posted all over town in one of the cities they brought the slaves through, turned into 'Johnny B. Goode.' "

After naming the song's protagonist Johnny after his keyboardist Johnnie Johnson, Berry wrote the lyrics in two weeks of "periodic application." The repeated chorus calls of "go Johnny go" are a tribute to Berry's mother's constant encouragement, while other imagery was also inspired by his family. "I'd been told my great grandfather lived 'way back up among the evergreens' in a log cabin,' " Berry writes. "I revived that era with a story about a 'colored boy name Johnny B. Goode'...but I thought that would seem biased to white fans...and changed it to 'country boy.' "

The single was recorded at Chess Studios in Chicago, on December 29 or 30, 1957, with Berry backed by a lean, swinging blues trio of Willie Dixon (bass), Lafayette Leake (piano) and Fed Below (drums). The same session also yielded "Reelin' and Rockin' " and "Sweet Little Sixteen." While those tunes also became standards, their impact pales in comparison to that of "Johnny B. Goode." As Billy Altman notes in his liner notes to *The Chuck Berry Box* (MCA, 1988), the song has become so ingrained in American culture that it's hard to imagine a time when it didn't exist. And, thanks to the late astronomer Carl Sagan, the whole universe may know the tune by now; it was hauled off on the Voyager 1 space probe, hurtling past Jupiter and Saturn and toward Neptune, some four billion miles away.

13. "TEXAS FLOOD"
Soloist: Stevie Ray Vaughan

Album: *Texas Flood* (Epic, 1983)

When Stevie Ray Vaughan and Double Trouble walked into Los Angeles' Down Town Studio in November 1982 to take advantage of 72 free hours of time offered by studio owner Jackson Browne, they had no idea they were about to start recording their debut album. "We were just making tape," recalls drummer Chris Layton. "We hoped that maybe we were making a demo that would actually be listened to by a real record company."

The first 24 hours were spent getting settled in L.A., and in the second and third days the band cut 10 songs—which became *Texas Flood*, in its entirety. "It really was just a big warehouse with concrete floors and some rugs thrown down," says bassist Tommy Shannon. "We just found a little corner, set up in a circle looking at and listening to each other and played like a live band." The trio recorded two songs the second day and eight the third—including "Texas Flood," a slow blues, written and recorded by the late Larry Davis in 1958, which had been a live staple of Vaughan's for years. It was the final tune recorded, cut in one take just before the free time ran out.

"That song and the whole first album captures the pure essence of what Stevie was all about," says Layton. "Countless people would tell Stevie how much they loved his guitar tone on *Texas Flood*. There was literally nothing between the guitar and the amp. It was just his number-one Strat plugged into a Dumble amp called Mother Dumble, which was owned by Jackson Browne and was just sitting in the studio. The real tone came from Stevie, and that whole recording was just so pure; the whole experience couldn't have been more innocent or naive. We were just playing. If we'd had known what was going to happen with it all, we might have screwed up. The magic was there and it came through on the tape. You can get most of what the band was ever about right there on that song and that album."

14. "LAYLA"
Soloists: Eric Clapton and Duane Allman

Album: Derek and the Dominos–*Layla and Other Assorted Love Songs* (Polydor, 1970)

Seven minutes of pure, quivering passion, "Layla" was Eric Clapton's magnificent scream of unrequited love for Patti Boyd, wife of his best friend—George Harrison.

"He grabbed one of my chicks," said Clapton of Harrison, "and so I thought I'd get even with him one day, on a petty level, and it grew from that. She was trying to attract his attention and so she used me, and I fell madly in love with her. [*Just*] listen to the words of 'Layla': 'I tried to give you consolation/When your old man had let you down/Like a fool, I fell in love with you/You turned my whole world upside down."

Clapton poured all of himself into "Layla," which he named after the classical Persian love poem, "The Story of Layla and the Majnun." The song began as a ballad, but quickly became a rocker, with Duane Allman reportedly coming up with the opening riff which would alter the tune. With Allman's majestic slide guitar prodding him on, Clapton unleashed some of his most focused, emotive playing.

"The song and the whole album is definitely equal parts Eric and Duane," says producer Tom Dowd, who introduced the two guitar titans, then sat back and watched them soar together. "There had to be some sort of telepathy going on because I've never seen spontaneous inspiration happen at that rate and level. One of them would play something, and the other reacted instantaneously. Never once did either of them have to say, 'Could you play that again, please?' It was like two hands in a glove. And they got tremendously off on playing with each other."

Nowhere was the interplay between Clapton and Allman more sublime than on "Layla," which, says Dowd, features six tracks of overlapping guitar: "There's an Eric rhythm part; three tracks of Eric playing harmony with himself on the main riff; one of Duane playing that beautiful bottleneck; and one of Duane and Eric locked up, playing countermelodies."

The tension of the main song finds release in a surging, majestic coda, which was recorded three weeks after the first part and masterfully spliced together by Dowd. The section begins with drummer Jim Gordon's piano part, echoed at various times by Clapton on the acoustic. Allman takes over with a celestial slide solo, beneath which Clapton plays a subtle countermelody. As the song fades out after a blissful climax, Allman has the last word, playing his signature "bird call" lick.

15 "HIGHWAY STAR"
Soloist: Ritchie Blackmore

Album: Deep Purple–*Machine Head* (Warner Bros., 1972)

"Highway Star" is but one highlight of *Machine Head,* Deep Purple's greatest triumph. Ironically, it almost never came to be. In early 1972, shortly after retreating to Montreaux, Switzerland, to record, the British band was beset by a wealth of problems. First, the place they were staying, which overlooked Lake Geneva, burned down—inspiring them to write "Smoke on the Water." Then, in response to a complaint about excessive noise, the police kicked the band out of the ballroom where they were recording.

"We were stuck in Switzerland with nowhere to go, and a friend of ours who was the mayor of the town said that there was an empty hotel we could use," recalls Ritchie Blackmore. "We gladly accepted and retreated to this lonely hotel in the mountains. We set up all the equipment in the corridor, with the drums and some amps tucked into alcoves.

"We had the Rolling Stones' mobile recording unit sitting outside in the snow, but to get there we had to run cable through two doors in the corridor into a room, through a bathroom and into another room, from which it went across a bed and out the veranda window, then ran along the balcony for about 100 feet and came back in through another bedroom window. It then went through that room's bathroom and into another corridor, then all the way down a marble staircase to the foyer reception area of the hotel, out the front door, across the courtyard and up the steps into the back of the mobile unit. I think that setup led to capturing some spontaneity, because once we got to the truck for a playback, even if we didn't think it was a perfect take, we'd go, 'Yeah, that's good enough.' Because we just couldn't stand going back again."

But while the vibe may have been loose, Blackmore's solo on 'Highway Star' was well planned. "I wrote that out note for note about a week before we recorded it," says the guitarist. "And that is one of the only times I have ever done that. I wanted it to sound like someone driving in a fast car, for it to be one of those songs you would listen to while speeding. And I wanted a very definite Bach sound, which is why I wrote it out—and why I played those very rigid arpeggios across that very familiar Bach progression—Dm, Gm, Cmaj, Amaj. I believe that I was the first person to do that so obviously on the guitar, and I believe that that's why it stood out and why people have enjoyed it so much.

"[*Keyboardist*] Jon Lord worked his part out to mine. Initially, I was going to play my solo over the chords he had planned out. But I couldn't get off on them, so I made up my own chords and we left the spot for him to write a melody. The keyboard solo is quite a bit more difficult than mine because of all those 16th notes. Over the years, I've always played that solo note for note—again, one of the few where I've done that—but it just got faster and faster onstage because we would drink more and more whiskey. Jon would have to play his already difficult part faster and faster and he would get very annoyed about it."

16. "HEARTBREAKER"
Soloist: Jimmy Page

Album: Led Zeppelin–*Led Zeppelin II* (Atlantic, 1969)

Performing a convincing solo in a group context is difficult for any musician, but it takes a real man to stand unaccompanied and deliver. On "Heartbreaker," Jimmy Page did just that. For an electrifying 45 seconds, Page let loose sans rhythm section and, needless to say, the guitar world has never been quite the same.

"I just fancied doing it," laughs Page. "I was always trying to do something different, or something no one else had thought of. But the interesting thing about that solo is that it was recorded after we had already finished "Heartbreaker"—it was an afterthought. That whole section was recorded in a different studio and was sort of slotted in the middle. If you notice, the whole sound of the guitar is different.

"The solo itself was made up on the spot. I think that was one of the first things I ever played through a Marshall. I was always having trouble with amps, and Marshalls were state-of-the-art reliability. By that time I was using a Les Paul, anyway, and that was just a classic setup."

"We definitely recorded the solo section separately," confirms engineer Eddie Kramer. "Jimmy walked in and set up and the whole session was over in about 20 minutes. He did two or three takes and we picked the best one, which was edited in later. However, to this day, I have a hard time listening to it, because I think we did a shitty edit—the difference in noise levels is pretty outrageous. But I don't think Jimmy cared, he was more interested in capturing an idea, and on that level, he succeeded."

17. "CLIFFS OF DOVER"
Soloist: Eric Johnson

Album: *Ah Via Musicom* (Capitol, 1990)

"I don't even know if I can take credit for writing 'Cliffs of Dover,' " says Eric Johnson of his best-known composition. "It was just there for me one day. There are songs I have spent months writing, and I literally wrote this one in five minutes. The melody was there in one minute and the other parts came together in another four. I think a lot of the stuff just comes through us like that. It's kind of a gift from a higher place that all of us are eligible for. We just have to listen for it and be available to receive it."

While it is true that he wrote the song in a blessed instant, the fact is that Johnson, a notoriously slow worker, took his time polishing it up to form. "It took me a while to achieve the facility to play it right," he says. "I was trying to work out the fingerings and how I wanted particular notes to hang over other notes."

Even allowing for Johnson's perfectionism, it took an extraordinarily long time for him to record a song that "came to him" in five minutes. That epiphany occurred in 1982, and within two years "Cliffs of Dover" was a popular staple of his live shows. He planned to include the song on his solo debut, *Tones* (Capitol, 1986), but, ironically, it didn't make the cut. "It was ousted by the people who were doing the record with me," Johnson explains. "I think they thought the melody was too straight or something."

Luckily, wiser heads prevailed on *Ah Via Musicom*. Though he had been playing "Cliffs of Dover" live for four or five years by then, it still took Johnson multiple takes to nail the song to his satisfaction—and he was never pleased with any version. "The whole solo is actually a composite of many guitar parts," Johnson says. "I knew exactly how I wanted it to sound—almost regal—and though I had versions that were close, none quite nailed it, so I kept playing around with different permutations of the many versions I had recorded until I got it just right.

"As a result, I actually ended up using two different-sounding guitars. Almost all of the song is a Gibson 335 through a Marshall, with an Echoplex and a tube driver. But in the middle of the solo there's 20 or 30 seconds played on a Strat. It really does sound different if you listen closely and at first I didn't think it could work, but I really liked this string of licks so we just decided to keep it. It basically sounds like I'm hitting a preamp box or switching amps.

"The difficulty on that song was to make the sound as clear as the melody is. It's just a simple little repeating melody, and for the song to work it had to be very up-front and crisp. Unfortunately, the G third on the guitar has a real tendency to waver and not be a smooth, clear note. As a result, I had to finger it just right—like a classical guitarist, using only the very tips of my fingers to achieve the best efficiency of my tonality. That's what took me so long: to be able to play all the fast licks with just the tips of my fingers, with just the right touch and tonality. Without a doubt, the most important thing is the song and melody, which in this case came very easily. But I like to do the best job I can of delivering it to the listener by the best possible way I can play it—and that came hard."

18. "LITTLE WING"
Soloist: Jimi Hendrix

Album: The Jimi Hendrix Experience–*Axis: Bold as Love* (Experience Hendrix/MCA, 1968)

Covered by artists like Eric Clapton, Stevie Ray Vaughan and Sting, "Little Wing" is one of Jimi Hendrix's most beautiful and enduring compositions. It's easy to see why. The original is seductively warm, poignant and light as a feather. Engineer Eddie Kramer explains how Jimi achieved the song's ethereal glow in the studio.

"One of my favorite touches on that track is the glockenspiel part, which was played by Jimi," says Kramer. "Part of the beauty of recording at Olympic Studios in London was using instruments that had been left from previous sessions. The glockenspiel was just laying around, so Jimi used it."

Hendrix's rich and watery guitar solo was, says Kramer, in part the product of a secret weapon. "One of the engineers had built this miniature Leslie," continues Kramer. "It was like it was built out of an Erector set and had a small eight-inch speaker that rotated. Believe it or not, the guitar solo was fed through this tiny thing, and that's the lovely effect you hear on the lead."

But for the true meaning of "Little Wing," it's best to go straight to the horse's mouth. " 'Little Wing' is like one of these beautiful girls that come around sometimes," explained Hendrix. "You ride into town for the drinks and parties and so forth. You play your gig; it's the same thing as the olden days. And these beautiful girls come around and really entertain you. You do actually fall in love with them because that's the only love you can have. It's not always the physical thing of 'Oh, there's one over there…' It's not one of those scenes. They actually tell you something. They release different things inside themselves, and then you feel to yourself, 'Damn, there's really a responsibility to some of these girls, you know, because they're the ones that are gonna get screwed.'

" 'Little Wing' was a very sweet girl that came around that gave me her whole life and more if I wanted it. And me with my crazy ass couldn't get it together, so I'm off here and there and off over there."

19. "FLOODS"
Soloist: Dimebag Darrell
Album: Pantera–*The Great Southern Trendkill* (Elektra, 1996)

"That particular solo was thought out in a more orchestrated fashion than some of the others I play where I just start ripping right off the bat," says Dimebag Darrell. "The thing that really makes the 'Floods' solo come across like it does is [bassist] Rex's playing behind it. He's using his fingers and he plays a whole bunch of cool licks and shit in there. He definitely adds to the vibe and feel of my lead because I'm playing off his part a lot—it was a great foundation for me to build on."

To fatten up the sound of the catchy arpeggiated theme that fills the first eight bars of his lead, Darrell doubled the part. "I picked up the idea of doubling from Randy Rhoads. It seemed appropriate to start off in a slow, melodic fashion and then build and build and build to the climax with the big harmonic squeals at the end. For that last big note I think there's four guitars going on. There's a squeal at the second fret of the G string, a squeal at the fifth fret of the G and then I used a DigiTech Whammy Pedal on two-string squeals at the harmonics at the fourth and 12th frets of the G and B strings, I believe. That was one of those deals where I didn't plan it out. I just sat there and fucked with it until it sounded right."

Adam Wilson/Retna

Dimebag Darrell

20. "BOHEMIAN RHAPSODY"
Soloist: Brian May

Album: Queen–*A Night at the Opera* (Hollywood, 1975)

"Freddie [*Mercury*] had the whole piece pretty well mapped out, as I remember, but he didn't have a guitar solo planned. So I guess I steamed in and said, 'This is the point where you need your solo, and these are the chords I'd like to use.' The chord progression for the solo is based on the verse, but with a slight foray into some different chords at the end, to make a transition into the next part of the song. I'd heard the track so many times while we were working on it that I knew in my head what I wanted to play for a solo. I wanted the guitar melody to be something extra, not just an echo of the vocal melody. I had a little tune in my head to play. It didn't take very long to record.

"The next section of the song, the heavy bit, was really part of Freddie's plan. I didn't change what he had very much. Those guitar riffs that everybody bangs their heads to are really more Freddie's than mine. And at the end of that section, I sort of took over. I wanted to do some guitar orchestrations—little violin lines—coming out of that. And it blended in very well with what Freddie was doing with the outro.

"We were stretching the limits of technology in those days. Since 'Bohemian Rhapsody' was entirely done on 16-track, we had to do a lot of bouncing as we went along; the tape got very thin. This 'legendary' story, which people think we made up, is true: we held the tape up to the light one day—we'd been wondering where all the top end was going—and what we discovered was virtually a transparent piece of tape. All the oxide had been rubbed off. It was time to hurriedly make a copy and get on with it."

21. "TIME"
Soloist: David Gilmour

Album: Pink Floyd–*Dark Side of the Moon* (Columbia, 1973)

"Working with Pink Floyd is an engineer's dream, so I tried to take advantage of the situation," says studio wizard Alan Parsons. "*Dark Side of the Moon* came at a crucial stage in my career, so I was highly motivated."

Parsons' attention to detail obviously paid off: He won a Grammy award for the best engineered album of 1973, and *DSOTM* went on to ride the charts for a record-breaking 14 years.

But while Parsons takes credit for many of *Moon*'s sonic innovations, he says the massive guitar sound on the album can be attributed to only one man: David Gilmour. "David was very much in control of his sound system," says Parsons. "We rarely added effects to his guitar in the control room. Generally speaking, the sound on the album is pretty much what came out of his amp. As I recall, he used a Hiwatt stack, a Fuzz Face and an Italian-made delay unit called a Binson Echorec."

Gilmour confirms: "For most of my solos, I usually use a fuzz box, a delay and a bright eq setting. But to get that kind of singing sustain, you really need to play loud—at or near the feedback threshold."

22. "SULTANS OF SWING"
Soloist: Mark Knopfler

Album: Dire Straits–*Dire Straits* (Warner Bros., 1978)

" 'Sultans of Swing' was originally written on a National Steel guitar in an open tuning, though I never performed it that way," recalls Mark Knopfler. "I thought it was dull, but as soon as I bought my first Strat in 1977, the whole thing changed, though the lyrics remained the same. It just came alive as soon as I played it on that '61 Strat—which remained my main guitar for many years and was basically the only thing I played on the first album—and the new chord changes just presented themselves and fell into place. It's really a good example of how the music you make is shaped by what you play it on, and is a lesson for young players. If you feel that you're not getting enough out of a song, change the instrument—go from an acoustic to an electric or vice versa, or try an open tuning. Do something to shake it up. As for the actual solo, it was just more or less what I played every night. It's just a Fender Twin and the Strat, with its three-way selector switch jammed into a middle position. That gives the song its sound, and I think there were quite a few five-way switches installed as a result of that song."

23. "BULLS ON PARADE"
Soloist: Tom Morello

Album: Rage Against the Machine–*Evil Empire* (Epic, 1996)

"That's me playing a solo by flicking the toggle switch back and forth," says Rage Against the Machine's innovative guitarist Tom Morello. "The story behind that sound starts with me going over to Ibanez one day. They were making a guitar for a guy in another band, and it had a special feature on it that they wanted me to try out. So I tried it, and it didn't really seem to do much that was anything different from a normal guitar. But I noticed that when you set the toggle between the two pickup settings, there was a really peculiar, high-pitched noise, and you could manipulate the tone of it dramatically when you turned the tone knob. I asked them what the noise was, and they said it was just incidental, that the guitar had an internal pickup and it was picking up this weird noise that they were trying to get rid of. I said, 'Oh, no, no—come here with that one.' [laughs] I gave them an idea of what I thought was possible with that noise, and they were kind enough to custom build a guitar for me with that feature in it."

24. "FADE TO BLACK"
Soloist: Kirk Hammett

Album: Metallica–*Ride the Lightning* (Elektra, 1984)

"I was still using my black Flying V on *Ride the Lightning,* but 'Fade to Black' sounds different—it has a warmer sound—because I used the neck pickup and played through a wah-wah pedal all the way in the 'up' position," says Kirk Hammett. "We wanted to double the first two solos and I did the first one no problem. But I had a much harder time doubling the second solo because it was slow and had a lot of space in it. Later, I realized that I actually harmonized it in a weird way—in minor thirds, major thirds and fifths. After cutting those two, I really wasn't sure what to play for the extended solo at the end. I was really bummed out because we had been in Denmark for five or six months, and I was very homesick; we were also having problems with our management. Because of that, and since it was a somber song anyway, I thought of very depressing things while I did the solo—and it really helped. We didn't double-track that solo, although I did play some arpeggios over the G-A-B progression. After that, I went back and did the clean guitar parts behind the verse, and James [*Hetfield*] played an arpeggiated figure while I arpeggiated three-note chords. The result was what I always have considered a very Dire Straits-type sound."

25. "AQUALUNG"
Soloist: Martin Barre

Album: Jethro Tull–*Aqualung* (Chrysalis, 1971)

"*Aqualung* was a difficult and very tense album to record, but at the end of the day it was important," says Jethro Tull guitarist Martin Barre. "Ian [*Anderson, vocals*] wrote the riff and verses to the song 'Aqualung,' but he felt it needed a new section for the guitar break. I said, 'Why don't we just play the verse chords in half-time for the first part of the solo, then pick it back up for the rest of the solo?' It was a simple solution that really worked.

"While I was playing the solo, which was really going well, Jimmy Page walked into the control room and started waving. I thought, Should I wave back and mess up the solo or should I just grin and carry on? Being a professional to the end, I just grinned."

26. "SMELLS LIKE TEEN SPIRIT"
Soloist: Kurt Cobain

Album: Nirvana–*Nevermind* (Geffen, 1991)

"I was trying to write the ultimate pop song," explained the late Kurt Cobain. "It's such a clichéd riff—it's so close to Boston's 'More Than a Feeling' riff or Richard Berry's 'Louie Louie.' When I came up with the guitar part, Krist [*Novoselic, bass*] looked at me and said, 'That's so ridiculous.' So I made the band play it for an hour and a half."

Niels Van Iperen/Retna

Kurt Cobain

27. "PRIDE AND JOY"
Soloist: Stevie Ray Vaughan

Album: *Texas Flood* (Epic, 1983)

"Pride and Joy" was recorded during the same 48-hour period as "Texas Flood"; both had been Vaughan live standbys for many years. "Stevie wrote 'Pride and Joy' for this new girlfriend he had when he was inspired by their relationship," says drummer Chris Layton. "Then they had a fight and he turned around and wrote 'I'm Cryin',' which is really the same song, just the flip side, lyrically."

When "Pride and Joy" was released as *Texas Flood*'s first single, it quickly put the then unknown Texas guitar slinger on the national blues-rock map. More cosmically, it also signaled that from-the-gut guitar music was not dead as a commercial and artistic force, no matter how many hits Culture Club and Flock of Seagulls had on *Solid Gold*. "When I heard that on the radio, I just said, 'Hallelujah,' " recalls Dickey Betts, whose Allman Brothers Band were prominent casualties of the age's anti-guitar disease. "He was just so good and strong and he would not be denied. He single handedly brought guitar and blues-oriented music back to the marketplace."

28. "MR. CROWLEY"
Soloist: Randy Rhoads

Album: Ozzy Osbourne–*Blizzard of Ozz* (Epic,1981)

"I'd have to say that 'Mr. Crowley' is my most memorable solo," said Randy Rhoads. "I had spent hours trying to figure out a solo for the song, but wasn't getting anywhere. I finally put something down. Then Ozzy came in and said, 'It's crap—everything you're playing is crap.' He told me to get in there and just play how I felt. He made me really nervous, so I just played anything. When I came back to listen to it, he said it was great, and I had to agree."

29. "FOR THE LOVE OF GOD"
Soloist: Steve Vai

Album: ***Passion and Warfare*** **(Epic, 1991)**

"The song is about how far people will go for the love of their god," says Steve Vai. "When you discipline yourself to quit smoking, to run faster or to play better, you have to reach deep down into a part of you. That is a profoundly spiritual event. That's when you come into contact with that little piece of God within you. That's what I was trying to achieve with 'For the Love of God'—I was trying to find that spot."

30. "SURFING WITH THE ALIEN"
Soloist: Joe Satriani

Album: ***Surfing with the Alien*** **(Epic, 1987)**

"We didn't know where that song was going until one afternoon when we went to record the melody and I plugged a wah-wah pedal and a Tubedriver into my 100-watt Marshall," says Joe Satriani. "Then, just on a whim, I said, 'Let's try this harmonizer.' It was one of those Eventide 949s. The sound that came out of the speakers blew us away so much that we recorded the melody and the solo in about a half-hour and sat back and went, 'Whoa! This is a song, man!'

"And then, of course, the Eventide broke down and we couldn't fix it. We couldn't do anything. We lost our tone. When we finally got it working again, we weren't able to re-create the original effect. It just sounded different. So rather than screw up a wonderful-sounding performance that may have had a couple of glitches, we decided to leave it, because it was just swinging.

"That wasn't the title track of the album for quite a while. It was going to be called *The Lord of Karma*. It wasn't until we finished that track and added the jet noises that we realized that 'Surfing' was the song that summed up the feeling of the whole album.

"The whole thing with putting the Silver Surfer on the cover was purely by accident. It came about because the product manager at the record label, Jim Kozlowski, used to be called the Silver Surfer when he was a DJ in Boston. When I delivered the album, he said, 'This is a great title. We should put the Silver Surfer on the cover.' I had no idea what he was talking about. I literally did not know anything about the comic book character."

31. "STRANGLEHOLD"
Soloist: Ted Nugent

Album: *Ted Nugent* (Epic, 1975)

" 'Stranglehold' is a masterpiece of jamology," proclaims Ted Nugent. "We were in the Sound Pit in Atlanta, Georgia, and I was showing my rhythm section of Cliff Davies [*drums*] and Rob De LaGrange [*bass*] the right groove for the song. I was playing my all-stock 1964 blonde Byrdland through four Fender Twin Reverbs and four Dual Showman bottoms on my rhythm settings—we were going to leave a hole there so that I could overdub a solo later. Then I started playing lead work, just kind of filling in and though I had never played those licks before in my life, they all just came to me. And because I got so inspired and because they followed me so perfectly, that demo is exactly what you hear on the record today. Take one, rhythm track is the song—it made such organic sense with the flow of music that I said, 'I'm not gonna fuck with that! That's it, baby.' And that is the essence of why people love it—because it is so spontaneous and uninhibited. The only thing we went back and overdubbed was Derek St. Holmes' vocals and my two tracks of harmonized feedback, which come in and out of the entire song. All the engineers and everyone kept saying, 'You can't do that, Ted.' And I said, 'Shut the fuck up!' Because I had the vision; I saw what the song could be, and I realized it."

32. "MACHINE GUN"
Soloist: Jimi Hendrix

Album: Band of Gypsys–*Band of Gypsys* (Experience Hendrix/MCA, 1970)

Contrary to popular belief, Hendrix was not in any kind of artistic decline during the last year of his life. In fact, it was quite the opposite. This apocalyptic performance of "Machine Gun," featuring Billy Cox on bass and Buddy Miles on drums, demonstrates that Jimi was still growing in leaps and bounds near the end. But while *Band of Gypsys* captures some of the guitarist's greatest improvisations to date, he was still dissatisfied with its outcome.

"I distinctly remember that Jimi wasn't particularly thrilled with *Band of Gypsys*," says engineer Eddie Kramer, who recorded the album and co-mixed and edited it with Hendrix. "He felt that Buddy Miles was trying to steal his thunder throughout the performance with his excessive scat singing. I can still see Jimi with his head buried in his arms, laying on the mixing console during playback, saying, 'Buddy, would you please just shut up!?' So, I would chop out huge passages of Buddy singing. And then I'd chop some more."

33. "THE THRILL IS GONE"

Soloist: B.B. King

Album: *Completely Well* (MCA, 1969)

"I carried this song around in my head for seven or eight years," B.B. King recalls about "The Thrill Is Gone," which had been an r&b hit for its author, pianist Roy Hawkins, in 1950. "It was a different kind of blues ballad. I'd been arranging it in my head and had even tried a couple of different versions that didn't work. But when I walked in to record on this night at the Hit Factory in New York, all the ideas came together. I changed the tune around to fit my style, and [*producer*] Bill Szymczyk set up the sound nice and mellow. We got through around 3 a.m. I was thrilled, but Bill wasn't, so I just went home. Two hours later, Bill called and woke me up and said, 'I think "The Thrill Is Gone" is a smash hit, and it would be even more of a hit if I added on strings. What do you think?' I said, 'Let's do it.' "

Strings in place, the song rose to number 15 on the *Billboard* chart, becoming King's first and only pop hit and earning him his first Grammy Award. "I felt especially proud because the song was true to me, and because Lucille is as much a part of it as me," King says. "She starts off singing and stays with me all the way until she takes the final bow. People ask why I don't sing and play at the same time, I've answered that I can't, but the deeper answer is that Lucille is one voice and I'm another. I hear those voices as distinct. One voice is coming through my throat, while the other is coming through my fingers. When one is singing, the other wants to listen."

34. "PARANOID ANDROID"
Soloist: Jonny Greenwood

Album: Radiohead–*OK Computer* (Capitol, 1997)

Radiohead consciously patterned their sprawling, epic song, "Paranoid Android," after the Beatles' "Happiness Is a Warm Gun." "It really started out as three separate songs and we didn't know what to do with them," explains singer/rhythm guitarist Thom Yorke. "Then we thought of 'Happiness'—which was obviously three different bits that John Lennon put together—and said, 'Why don't we try that?' " Still, the song wasn't really complete until lead player Jonny Greenwood added a fourth section as a fade out—a lengthy, intense solo which alternates between being backward and forward. "It was something I had floating around for a while and the song needed a certain burn," recalls Greenwood. "I don't usually have stockpiles of riffs lying around, but this happened to be the right key and the right speed and it fit right in."

35. "CEMETERY GATES"
Soloist: Dimebag Darrell

Album: Pantera–*Cowboys from Hell* (Elektra, 1990)

"I got home with a pretty good buzz on, picked up my ax, turned on the four-track, cranked it loud as hell with the loose buzz theory that anything and everything goes, and just played it," Dimebag recalls. "I played three solos back-to-back, didn't bother listening to 'em and crashed out not so happy. The next morning I woke up thinking I had a lot of work to do...I almost started from scratch but then decided to slow down and listen. So I fired up my four-track, put my ears on and bam! Lo and behold, there it was! The first lead I played the night before was it for sure. Hey man, the second and third weren't bad, but the first had that first-take magic! I didn't touch it."

36. "BLACK STAR"
Soloist: Yngwie Malmsteen

Album: *Rising Force* (Polydor, 1984)

"I've been playing that song, or variations of it, since I was a teenager in Sweden," Yngwie Malmsteen recently told his fan club. "I used to play really long, uninterrupted improvisations when I played local shows in Stockholm back then, and it developed from that. I didn't sit down and actually write out the notes for it; when I'm feeling inspired, the music just flows out of me. It's in my head and my ears and flows out of my fingers."

"Black Star" flew through Malmsteen's fingers on his solo debut album, recorded in 1984 at Rocshire Studios in Anaheim, California, with the guitarist producing as well as playing bass and, of course, all guitar parts. "We recorded all the basic tracks and then Yngwie had to go on the road with Alcatrazz," recalls keyboardist Jens Johansson. "He flew in here and there to do overdubs. There are probably three guitar tracks on 'Black Star,' and I remember watching Yngwie doing them and being blown away at how he could effortlessly synchronize the vibrato if he was overdubbing a harmony. It all happened pretty fast and on 'Black Star,' especially, he knew what he wanted it to sound like. And he got it."

37. "SWEET CHILD O' MINE"
Soloist: Slash

Album: Guns N' Roses–*Appetite for Destruction* (Geffen, 1987)

"When 'Sweet Child O' Mine' was written, it was a joke as far as I was concerned," says Slash. "I was just fuckin' around when I came up with that riff. To me it was a nightmare because, for some strange reason, everyone picked up on it and, the next thing you knew, it had turned into a song. I hated it forever! The guitar solo itself is a one-take, spontaneous kind of thing. Having played the song at rehearsals enough times, when it came to recording it I knew exactly where the melody was and it came real easy."

38. "WHOLE LOTTA LOVE"
Soloist: Jimmy Page

Album: Led Zeppelin–*Led Zeppelin II* (Atlantic, 1969)

"I used distant miking to get that rhythm guitar tone," says Jimmy Page. "Miking used to be a science, and I'd heard that distance makes depth, which in turn gives you a fatter guitar sound. The amp was turned up very high. It was distorting, just controlled to the point where it had some balls to it. I also used a depressed wah-wah pedal on the solo, as I did on 'Communication Breakdown.' It gets you a really raucous sound. The descending riff that answers the line 'whole lotta love' was created using slide and backward echo. Backward echo has been used a lot now, but I think I was the first to use it."

39. "CORTEZ THE KILLER"
Soloist: Neil Young

Album: *Zuma* (Reprise, 1975)

"Cortez the Killer" hails from *Zuma*, one of Neil Young's most overlooked albums, often lost in the shuffle of its predecessor, the much-praised *Tonight's the Night*, which came out just five months prior. But there's really a very simple explanation for the song's high rating. Just take it from Young himself, who once proclaimed that, " 'Cortez' is some of my best guitar playing ever!"

Remarkably, the song's structure was largely shaped by an accident—a power failure which occurred in the midst of recording a perfect, transcendent take of the song. Rather than recut the tune, Young just plowed forward and later he and producer David Briggs went back and did some creative editing, which required the lopping off of several verses. "They missed a whole verse, a whole section!" Young says. "You can hear the splice on the recording where we stop and start again. It's a messy edit...incredible! It was a total accident. But that's how I see my best art, as one magical accident after another. That's what is so incredible."

"Cortez the Killer," about the Spanish explorer who conquered Mexico with bloody success, is also a prime example of Young's physical style of lead playing.

"I am a naturally very destructive person," he says. "And that really comes out in my guitar playing. Man, if you think of guitar playing in terms of boxing...well, let's just say I'm not the kind of guitarist you'd want to play against. I'm just scarred by life. Nothing in particular. No more scarred than anyone else. Only other people often don't let themselves know how damaged they are, like I do, and deal with it."

40. "REELIN' IN THE YEARS"

Soloist: Elliott Randall

Album: Steely Dan—*Can't Buy a Thrill* (MCA, 1972)

While recording Steely Dan's 1972 debut, Walter Becker and Donald Fagen knew they had a great track for "Reelin' in the Years"—if they could only come up with the appropriate guitar solo to jumpstart the tune. So they put in a call to Elliott Randall, with whom they had worked in the backing band for Jay and the Americans, and who had played on many of the duo's early, pre-Steely Dan demos.

"They were having trouble finding the right 'flavor' solo for 'Reelin',' and asked me to give it a go," recalls Randall. "Most of the song was already complete, so I had the good fortune of having a very clear picture of what the solo was laying on top of. They played it for me without much dialogue about what I should play. It just wasn't necessary because we did it in one take and nothing was written. Jeff Baxter played the harmony parts, but my entire lead—intro/answers/solo/end solo—was one continuous take played through a very simple setup: my old Strat, the same one I've been using since 1965, plugged directly into an Ampeg SVT amp, and miked with a single AKG 414. The whole solo just came to me, and I feel very fortunate to have been given the opportunity to play it."

41. "BRIGHTON ROCK"

Soloist: Brian May

Album: Queen–*Sheer Heart Attack* (Elektra, 1974)

Universally venerated for his lavish guitar orchestrations and tasteful British restraint, Brian May kicked over the traces on this high energy rocker that leads off Queen's third album, *Sheer Heart Attack*. One of May's most blues-based excursions ever, the song's extended solo section grew out of the guitarist's experiments with an Echoplex tape delay unit. His original goal was to reproduce his multi-part guitar harmonies live onstage with Queen, back in the days before harmonizers were invented.

"I started messing around with the Echoplex, the delay that was available at the time," May recalls. "I turned up the regeneration until it was giving me multiple repeats. I discovered you could do a lot with this—you could set up rhythms and play against them, or you could play a line and then play a harmony to it. But I decided that the delay [times] I wanted weren't available on the Echoplex. So I modified it and made a new rail, which meant I could slide the head along and make the delay any length I wanted, because the physical distance between the two heads is what gave you the delay. Eventually, I had two home-adapted Echoplexes. And I discovered that if you put each echo through its own amp, you wouldn't have any nasty interference between the two signals. Each amp would be like a full-blown, sustaining, overdriven guitar which didn't have anything to do with the other one.

"So, 'Brighton Rock' was the first time that got onto a record. I'd already been trying it live onstage in the middle of 'Son and Daughter' [*from Queen's self-titled '73 debut album*], when Queen first toured with Mott the Hoople. It was rather crude at first. But I certainly had a lot of fun with it."

42. "WHILE MY GUITAR GENTLY WEEPS"

Soloist: Eric Clapton

Album: The Beatles–*The Beatles* (Capitol, 1968)

"When we actually started recording this, it was just me playing the acoustic guitar and singing it, and nobody was interested," recalls the song's author, George Harrison. "Well, Ringo probably was, but John and Paul weren't. When I went home that night, I was really disappointed because I thought, Well, this is really quite a good song; it's not as if it's crap! And the next day I happened to drive back into London with Eric [*Clapton*], and I suddenly said, 'Why don't you come play on this track?' And he said, 'Oh, I couldn't do that; the others wouldn't like it…' But I finally said, 'Well, damn, it's my song, and I'd like you to come down.' So he did, and everybody was good as gold because he was there. I sang it with the acoustic guitar with Paul on piano, and Eric and Ringo. Later, Paul overdubbed bass. Then we listened back to it and Eric said, 'Ah, there's a problem, though; it's not Beatlesy enough.' So we put the song through the ADT [*automatic double tracker*] to wobble it a bit."

43. "SHARP DRESSED MAN"

Soloist: Billy Gibbons

Album: ZZ Top–*Eliminator* (Warner Bros., 1983)

In 1983, a smart gambling man would have bet the house on ZZ Top's imminent doom. After all, it wasn't the best of times for good and greasy Texas blues and boogie music. Then the Little Old Band from Texas surprised everyone with *Eliminator*, a brilliant merger of roadhouse blues and synthesizer swells and looped beats. The album quickly became their biggest hit ever, spurred in large part by the irresistible "Sharp Dressed Man."

"That song and the whole album really embrace the simplicity of blues and techno music with the complex challenge of how to blend them together," says guitarist Billy Gibbons. "If you zero in on the middle solo, you will find a slide guitar part played in open E tuning on a Fender Esquire and a sudden shift halfway through the solo to standard Spanish electric tuning played on my good ol' Les Paul, Pearly Gates. Both were played through a Marshall plexi 100-watt head with two angled cabinets with Celestion 25-watt greenbacks. It was a compound track, two parts blended to one.

"To this day, the song certainly stands among one of the band's favorites and we're particularly delighted to share spotlight on a solo that enjoys such favoritism. There are, of course, the more intricate and demanding solos, but we will gladly finger through the solo of 'Sharp Dressed Man' at any requested moment! The track just has a really raucous delivery, which is a good ignition point onstage, sitting on the tailgate out in the middle of nowhere, sipping a cold one, or wherever you may be. It just does something to you."

44. "ALIVE"
Soloist: Mike McCready

Album: Pearl Jam–*Ten* (Epic, 1991)

"Basically, I copied Ace Frehley's solo from 'She,' " says Pearl Jam guitarist Mike McCready. "Which, of course, was copied from Robby Krieger's solo in the Doors' 'Five to One.' "

45. "LIGHT MY FIRE"
Soloist: Robby Krieger

Album: The Doors–*The Doors* (Elektra, 1967)

"Light My Fire" was one of the first songs ever written by Robby Krieger, and his extended solo on the album version was also one of his shining moments as a guitarist. Ironically, however, in order for "Light My Fire" to become a hit for the Doors and Krieger the songwriter, Krieger the guitarist had to swallow his pride and allow his masterly two-and-a-half-minute solo to be trimmed down to its essential opening and closing themes for use on the single.

"That always bothered me," Krieger readily admits. "We never wanted to cut it, but our first single, 'Break on Through,' flopped and radio stations told us that 'Light My Fire' would be a hit if we cut it down. We didn't have much choice because AM radio ruled everything, and if you wanted to get on AM you had to have a short song."

The longer solo now regularly broadcast on the radio in its entirety is a perfect distillation of Krieger's style. A flamenco-trained guitarist who played with his fingers and often evoked sitar-like Eastern sounds with his Gibson SG, Krieger pulled out all the stops on "Light My Fire." Still, the guitarist says that the complete version on the album is far from his finest effort. "It was the kind of solo that I usually did, but it was different every night. To be honest, the one on the album is not one of my better takes. I only had two tries at it. But it's not bad; I'm glad that it was as good as it was."

46. "HOT FOR TEACHER"
Soloist: Edward Van Halen

Album: Van Halen–*1984* (Warner Bros., 1984)

"I winged that one," says Eddie Van Halen. "If you listen to it, the timing changes in the middle of nowhere. We were in a room playing together and I kind of winked at the guys and said, 'Okay, we're changing now!' Because I don't count, I just follow my feelings. I tend to do a lot of things in threes and fives, instead of fours.

"My weird sense of time just drives my brother Alex nuts because he's a drummer, so he has to count. But generally he'll say, 'Well, Ed, you did it in five again. If that's the way you want it…' But that's not the way I want it, that's just what feels right to me."

47. "JESSICA"
Soloist: Dickey Betts

Album: The Allman Brothers Band–*Brothers and Sisters* (Polydor, 1974)

Dickey Betts' instrumental "Jessica" is as uplifting a piece of music as can be found in all rock. And that, says Betts, is no coincidence: the music actually began with his desire to express pure jubilation.

"My instrumentals try to create some of the basic feelings of human interaction, like anger and joy and love," says Betts. "With

'Jessica,' I knew what I wanted to do, but I couldn't quite find it. Then my little daughter, Jessica, crawled into the room, and I just started playing to her, trying to capture the feeling of her crawling and smiling. That's why I named it after her."

Betts wrote the song's melodic theme while emulating one of his heroes—the gypsy guitarist Django Reinhardt, who had the use of only two fingers on his left hand. "I came up with that melody using just two fingers as a sort of tribute to Django," says Betts. "That the song turned out so well is very satisfying. In general, writing a good instrumental is very fulfilling, because you've transcended language and spoken to someone with a melody."

48. "SYMPATHY FOR THE DEVIL"
Soloist: Keith Richards

Album: Rolling Stones–*Beggar's Banquet* (Abkco, 1968)

Writer Stanley Booth once suggested to Keith Richards that "Sympathy for the Devil" was cut from the same cloth as bluesman Robert Johnson's haunting "Me and the Devil Blues." "Yeah," Richards replied. "All of us pursued by the same demon." But while "Sympathy's" lyrics reflect the Stones' attraction to the dark side and allegiance to Johnson, the music is a prime example of how in a real band, composition is a group effort. "It started as sort of a folk song with acoustics and ended up as kind of a mad samba, with me playing bass and overdubbing the guitar later," says Richards. "That's why I don't like to go into the studio with all the songs worked out and planned beforehand. Because you can write the songs, but you've got to give the band something to use its imagination on as well. That can make a very ordinary song come alive into something totally different. You can write down the notes being played, but you can't put down the X factor—so important in rock and roll—which is the feel."

49. "EUROPA"
Soloist: Carlos Santana

Album: *Amigos* (Columbia, 1976)

"I started writing this song in 1966 or '67, but didn't finish it until '75 when we were on tour with Earth, Wind and Fire, in Manchester, England," says Carlos Santana. "We were backstage while they were onstage playing. And we were just warming up, tuning up. I started playing it and [*keyboardist*] Tom Coster and I completed it right there on the spot. It immediately became a crowd favorite; it is one of those songs that, whether it's played in Japan or in Jerusalem or in South America, it just fits right in with everything."

50. "SHOCK ME"
Soloist: Ace Frehley

Album: Kiss–*Alive II* (Mercury, 1977)

"I basically did the same solo every night on that tour, with minor alterations, so I had it kind of planned out when I did it the night we recorded it live for *Alive II*," says Ace Frehley.

"But if you listen carefully to the 'Shock Me' solo you can hear me make a mistake about two thirds of the way through. Instead of tapping a B at the 19th fret of the high E string, I accidentally hit the A# note at the 18th fret—that's definitely a wrong note for the scale I'm using. We could have fixed it in the mix, but I said to Eddie [*Kramer,* Alive II *producer*], 'Screw it! Leave it in. The run sounds cool, so who cares—it's rock and roll!' "

51. "NO MORE TEARS"
Soloist: Zakk Wylde

Album: Ozzy Osbourne–*No More Tears* (Epic, 1991)

R. Collaris/Sunshine/Retna

Ace Frehley

52. "STAR SPANGLED BANNER"

Soloist: Jimi Hendrix

Album: *The Ultimate Experience* (MCA, 1993)

53. "TOO ROLLING STONED"
Soloist: Robin Trower

Album: *Bridge of Sighs* (Chrysalis, 1974)

54. "GEEK USA"
Soloist: Billy Corgan

Album: Smashing Pumpkins–*Siamese Dream* (Virgin, 1993)

55. "SATCH BOOGIE"
Soloist: Joe Satriani

Album: *Surfing with the Alien* (Epic, 1988)

56. "WAR PIGS"
Soloist: Tony Iommi

Album: Black Sabbath–*Paranoid* (Warner Bros., 1970)

57. "WORKING MAN"
Soloist: Alex Lifeson

Album: Rush–*Rush* (Mercury, 1974)

58. "COCAINE"
Soloist: Eric Clapton

Album: *Slowhand* (Polydor, 1977)

59. "YOU REALLY GOT ME"
Soloist: Dave Davies

Album: The Kinks–*You Really Got Me* (Reprise, 1965)

60. "ZOOT ALLURES"
Soloist: Frank Zappa

Album: *Zoot Allures* (Warner Bros., 1976)

61. "MASTER OF PUPPETS"
Soloist: Kirk Hammett

Album: Metallica–*Master of Puppets* (Elektra, 1986)

62. "MONEY"
Soloist: David Gilmour

Album: Pink Floyd–*Dark Side of the Moon* (Capitol, 1973)

63. "SCAR TISSUE"
Soloist: John Frusciante

Album: Red Hot Chili Peppers–*Californication* (Warner Bros., 1999)

64. "LITTLE RED CORVETTE"
Soloist: Dez Dickerson

Album: Prince–*1999* (Warner Bros., 1982)

65. "BLUE SKY"
Soloists: Duane Allman and Dickey Betts

Album: The Allman Brothers Band–*Eat a Peach* (Polydor, 1972)

66. "THE NUMBER OF THE BEAST"
Soloists: Dave Murray and Adrian Smith

Album: Iron Maiden–*The Number of the Beast* (Castle, 1982)

67. "BEAT IT"
Soloist: Eddie Van Halen

Album: Michael Jackson–*Thriller* (Epic, 1982)

68. "STARSHIP TROOPER"
Soloist: Steve Howe

Album: Yes–*The Yes Album* (Atlantic, 1971)

69. "AND YOUR BIRD CAN SING"
Soloist: George Harrison

Album: The Beatles–*Revolver* (Parlophone, 1966)

70. "PURPLE HAZE"
Soloist: Jimi Hendrix

Album: *Are You Experienced?* (MCA, 1967)

71. "(DON'T FEAR) THE REAPER"
Soloist: Donald "Buck Dharma" Roeser

Album: Blue Oyster Cult–*Maggot Brain* (Columbia, 1976)

72. "WALK THIS WAY"
Soloist: Joe Perry

Album: Aerosmith–*Toys in the Attic* (Columbia, 1975)

73. "STASH"
Soloist: Trey Anastasio

Album: Phish–*Picture of Nectar* (Elektra, 1991)

74. "LAZY"
Soloist: Ritchie Blackmore

Album: Deep Purple–*Machine Head* (Warner Bros., 1972)

75. "WON'T GET FOOLED AGAIN"
Soloist: Pete Towshend

Album: The Who–*Who's Next* (MCA, 1971)

76. "CINNAMON GIRL"
Soloist: Neil Young

Album: Neil Young & Crazy Horse–
Everybody Knows This Is Nowhere (Reprise, 1969)

77. "MAN IN THE BOX"
Soloist: Jerry Cantrell

Album: Alice in Chains–*Facelift* (Columbia, 1990)

78. "TRUCKIN' "
Soloist: Jerry Garcia

Album: Grateful Dead–*American Beauty/*
Workingman's Dead (Warner Bros., 1970)

79. "MEAN STREET"
Soloist: Eddie Van Halen

Album: Van Halen–*Fair Warning* (Warner Bros., 1981)

80. "YOU SHOOK ME ALL NIGHT LONG"
Soloist: Angus Young

Album: AC/DC–*Back in Black* (Elektra, 1980)

81. "SWEET JANE"
Soloist: Lou Reed

Album: Velvet Underground–*Loaded* (Warner Bros., 1970)

82. "21ST CENTURY SCHIZOID MAN"
Soloist: Robert Fripp

Album: King Crimson–*In the Court of the Crimson King* (Atlantic, 1969)

83. "SCUTTLE BUTTIN' "
Soloist: Stevie Ray Vaughan

Album: *Couldn't Stand the Weather* (Epic, 1984)

84. "LIGHTS OUT"
Soloist: Michael Schenker

Album: UFO–*Lights Out* (Capitol, 1977)

85. "MOONAGE DAYDREAM"
Soloist: Mick Ronson

Album: David Bowie–*The Rise and Fall of Ziggy Stardust and the Spiders from Mars* (RCA, 1972)

86. "WHIPPING POST"
Soloist: Duane Allman and Dickey Betts

Album: The Allman Brothers Band–
The Allman Brothers Band (Atco, 1969)

87. "HIGHWAY 61 REVISITED"
Soloist: Johnny Winter

Album: Johnny Winter–*Second Winter* (Columbia, 1969)

88. "KID CHARLEMAGNE"
Soloist: Larry Carlton

Album: Steely Dan–*The Royal Scam* (MCA, 1976)

89. "KILLING IN THE NAME"
Soloist: Tom Morello

Album: Rage Against the Machine–
Rage Against the Machine (Epic, 1992)

90. "HOLY WARS...THE PUNISHMENT DUE"
Soloist: Marty Friedman

Album: Megadeth–*Rust in Peace* (Capitol, 1990)

91. "HEARD IT THROUGH THE GRAPEVINE"

Soloist: John Fogerty

Album: Creedence Clearwater Revival–*Cosmo's Factory* (Fantasy, 1970)

92. "STRAY CAT STRUT"

Soloist: Brian Setzer

Album: Stray Cats–*Built for Speed* (EMI, 1982)

93. "THE END"

Soloist: Robby Krieger

Album: The Doors–*The Doors* (Elektra, 1967)

94. "MR. SCARY"

Soloist: George Lynch

Album: Dokken–*Back for the Attack* (Elektra, 1987)

95. "YELLOW LEDBETTER"

Soloist: Mike McCready

Album: Pearl Jam–*Jeremy CD single* (Epic, 1994)

96. "HONKY TONK WOMAN"
Soloist: Keith Richards

Album: Rolling Stones–*Hot Rocks 1964–1971* (London, 1972)

97. "BEYOND THE REALMS OF DEATH"
Soloist: Glenn Tipton

Album: Judas Priest–*Stained Class* (Columbia, 1978)

98. "UNDER A GLASS MOON"
Soloist: John Petrucci

Album: Dream Theater–*Images & Words* (Atlantic, 1992)

99. " 'CAUSE WE'VE ENDED AS LOVERS"
Soloist: Jeff Beck

Album: *Blow by Blow* (Epic, 1975)

100. "WANTED DEAD OR ALIVE"
Soloist: Richie Sambora

Album: Bon Jovi–*Slippery When Wet* (Mercury, 1986)

Guitar World, May 1996

The Dirty Dozen

Guitar World's Guide to the 12 Greatest Guitar Sounds of All Time.

There are electric guitar sounds. Then there are *electrifying* guitar sounds—the dozen or so guitar tones that define our sense of what rock is and what it feels like. Such sounds are like the energy that crackles through a room when an incredibly attractive or charismatic person walks in the door, or the tension that grips our throats when we feel that some supernatural phenomenon is about to occur. We sense that we are in the presence of something far bigger than ourselves—the presence of greatness.

Truly grasping the tones of masters like Jimi Hendrix, Jeff Beck or Stevie Ray Vaughan in all their gnarly detail would take a lifetime of study. To help you along the way, *Guitar World* has painstakingly crafted technical road maps to 12 of the most earth-shaking guitar sounds of all time. We hope that these sonic secrets will point you in the right direction in your own quest for finding the ultimate tone.

Black Sabbath's TONY IOMMI

Album: *Paranoid*
Studio: Regent Sound, England
Producer: Rodger Bain

Black Sabbath's first album may be the prototypical heavy metal album, but their second album, *Paranoid*, is the production model upon which the genre was built. Songs like "Paranoid," "War Pigs" and "Iron Man" made other hard rock bands sound downright quaint by comparison. The heart of Black Sabbath's sound was Tony Iommi's crunchy, distorted power chords and fat, nimble leads, which made Ozzy Osbourne's nasal, monotone vocals sound nasty and menacing.

Paranoid was recorded over the course of a few days in a tiny eight-track studio at Regent Sound. Iommi explains that most of the finished recordings are first takes that were played live in the studio.

Jeff Davy/Retna

Tony Iommi

"It was like recording in a garage," he notes. "We stuck a mic in front of my cabinet, and I played the original track with the band, did an overdub and that was it. To us it was like going to a gig. We thought that a couple of days was plenty of time to record and mix an album."

In the late Sixties, as now, Marshall amplifiers ruled the rock world, but Iommi broke from convention by using Laney amps. "The reason's quite simple," explains Iommi. "Laney was from Birmingham, and so were we. They were a new company that started out at about the same time that we did, in 1968. They were very helpful to us, and we worked together. They gave us all the amplification we needed. I'm still using Laneys, though now I've got my own signature model."

For *Paranoid*, Iommi plugged his Gibson SG into a 100-watt Laney head and a single 4 x 12 Laney cabinet. The real secret to his tone, however, was a modified Rangemaster treble booster that he used to overdrive the amp's input. "The problem in those days was that you had to use your straight head and there was nothing to boost it," he recalls. "I spoke to this electronics guy, and he said, 'Oh, I could do something with that treble booster.' He modified it, and it worked out really well. It really did the job for me. I used that for 15 years before somebody lost it. I worked with companies for many years, trying to get them to build that kind of thing in their amplifiers, and they said, 'No, it will distort! You can't have that.' But that was the point! Of course, many years later they decided to do it."

The Gibson SG, which has long been associated with Iommi, became his instrument of choice by accident. "I was using a Fender Stratocaster when we were recording the first album," he notes. "I used it on 'Wicked World,' and then the pickup broke right after we finished recording it. In those days you couldn't get any replacement pickups. My SG was my second guitar. It was always sitting around, and I never really played it. All of a sudden I had to get used to it. I used it ever since and have never looked back."

EDWARD VAN HALEN

Album: *Van Halen*
Studio: Sunset Sound, Hollywood
Producer: Ted Templeman

For most of the Seventies, Southern California's musical climate was characterized by sunny, laid-back music such as Linda Rondstadt and Fleetwood Mac's folk-pop and the Eagles' cocaine-cowboy rock. But when Van Halen unchained its debut album in 1978, those sunny skies became obscured by clouds of big hair as a torrent of metal bands flooded Sunset Strip nightclubs, all trying to ride the wave of Van Halen's success.

The ominous sound of Edward Van Halen's guitar on those 10 timeless tracks hit guitarists the same way Hendrix's "Purple Haze" affected players a decade earlier. "Eruption," featuring Eddie's revolutionary fretboard fireworks, confounded many critics who thought it was some kind of synthesizer solo or studio trickery. But despite all the mythology and mystery that's been perpetuated about it throughout the years, Van Halen's equipment wasn't much different from rigs used by other guitarists at the time.

"I plugged an old 100-watt Marshall Super Lead through a 4 x 12 cabinet for that album," says Eddie. "It's a '66 or '67—nothing special. I've done all the Van Halen records with that same amp. We miked it with two Shure SM-57s—one directly in the middle of the cone and one angled to the side to get a little more meat out of it."

Eddie's main guitar was a homemade solidbody, which he constructed from a Boogie Bodies neck and body, Gibson frets, a Fender Strat tremolo and a Gibson PAF humbucker. "It was neat," he recalls. "I really felt I was onto something when I built that guitar, because you couldn't buy anything like it at the time." On the tracks that didn't require any tremolo acrobatics, he played an Ibanez Destroyer (a copy of a late-Fifties, Korina Gibson Explorer) that he retrofitted with PAF humbuckers. "You can hear that on 'Jamie's Cryin',' 'On Fire' and 'You Really Got Me,' " says Eddie. "It was a great-sounding guitar, but I fucked it up by cutting a big chunk out of it later. It never sounded the same again." Eddie doubled his "Ain't Talkin' 'Bout Love" solo with a Coral electric sitar.

One key element of Van Halen's early tone was an original, script-logo MXR Phase 90 that he often stomped on for his solos. The effect can be heard on "Eruption," "Ice Cream Man," "You Really Got Me" and the intro to "Atomic Punk." Other effects he employed included an MXR flanger, an Echoplex and a Univox EC-80 echo used exclusively to generate the octave divebomb at the end of "Eruption."

In early interviews, Eddie often remarked that his amps were heavily modified, but he recently debunked that myth by admitting that his amps are stock. However, he still maintains that he connected a Variac (a device that controls the amount of voltage coming from an AC outlet) to his amps. "The only way I can make my Marshall work is with everything turned all the way up," he explains. "When we played in clubs, it would be too loud and the amp would feed back. I tried using a light dimmer, but it fried a fuse when I hooked it up to the house. So I went down to Radio Shack and bought a Variac, which worked. I always used it for recording in the early days before I started sitting in the control room. Whenever the amp would feed back, I'd turn it down with the Variac."

Producer Ted Templeman panned Eddie's main guitar part to the left channel in the mix, allowing guitarists to glom Eddie's performance in its full glory. "I hated that," Eddie squawks. "When the left back speaker in your car is blown, the guitar is gone!"

STEVIE RAY VAUGHAN

Album: *In Step*
Studio: Kiva, Memphis
Producers: Jim Gaines and Stevie Ray Vaughan

Like a tangy Texas barbecue sauce, the tasty guitar tone served up by Stevie Ray Vaughan on his *In Step* album was comprised of many ingredients. Foremost was Vaughan himself. Then there was his beloved hybrid Number One guitar, comprised of a '63 Strat neck on a '59 Strat body—its sunburst finish all but completely worn away. The Strat was plugged into a stockpile of amps and pedals, based on the late guitarist's live rig. Luckily, producer Jim Gaines remembers the recipe: "Stevie Ray would use two Ibanez Tube Screamers together and two wah-wah pedals. Those were his only pedals."

The signal from Stevie's guitar was routed via a series of splitter boxes to eight different amps stacked in the main room at Kiva, a Memphis studio. "We called it the Wall of Doom," says Gaines, laughing. "He had Dumbles, Marshalls and Fender Bassmans, Supers and Quad Reverbs [*a relatively obscure Seventies Fender amp with four 12-inch speakers*]. He used different combinations of them, depending on the kind of sound he wanted."

Gaines got the sound on tape using a combination of close miking and stereo distant miking, using a mixture of Shure SM-57s, Sennheiser 421s and the occasional AKG 414 for extra brightness on a particular amp. "When Stevie cut a live guitar part, it would go down to anywhere from eight to 10 different tracks. Sometimes I'd have to rely on the room mikes because of weird phasing problems with the individual amp mikes. Depending on what kind of sound we wanted, I'd position the stereo mikes anywhere from six to 10 feet in front of the amps, trying to capture where the convergence points were coming off this big wall of speakers."

Two additional amps were placed in an isolation booth: a vintage, trapezoidal-shaped Gibson stereo amp with an angled speaker arrangement, and a Vibratone—a small Leslie-style amp. "Those amps would have been blown out of the room if we'd put them in with the others," Gaines explains, "so we had to isolate them. Stevie didn't want to use many effects in the mixing. For chorusing effects, we'd use the Vibratone. We put a Variac on it to vary the speed, so the chorusing would be in time with the song. That amp went on a separate track. I miked it in stereo, using two 57s, to further enhance the chorusy sound. Then, if we wanted any additional chorusing, Stevie would use an old Roland Dimension D. That was basically the sound of the album."

Soundgarden's KIM THAYIL

Album: *Badmotorfinger*
Studio: Bad Animals, Seattle
Producer: Terry Date

When Soundgarden set out in 1991 to record the pivotal *Badmotorfinger*, the last thing on Kim Thayil's mind was creating a stylized tone that would become one of the most imitated guitar sounds of the Nineties. "I was trying to get a low, heavy sound while at the same time getting it to cut through," says Thayil. "I was into Metallica's sound back then, the Melvins, too, and wanted to achieve that same overwhelming heaviness."

He succeeded. With his beloved "Spider-man" Guild S-1 (customized with a sticker Kim found in a cereal box) pumped through his mainstay Peavey VTM setup, Thayil instinctively zeroes in on the earth-plowing sound by employing the now-famous dropped-D tuning and adjusting the amplifier's bottom end. "The VTMs have this circuitry where you can boost the lows," says Thayil. "I had it cranked. That sound has a good feel to it and good boom, which is great for muting. It also has a nice, full lead tone and a warm low end that is good for vibrato."

Unaware he was spearheading a tonal renaissance, Thayil attained a finished guitar sound that relied less on studio magic and more on a necessity to accommodate his love for feedback and sustain. "I like to get a big guitar sound for melodies and vibratos and to get a lead sound that's fat and has sustain."

Imitated to the point of cookie-cutter absurdity, Thayil weighs the pros and cons of Soundgarden's guitar influence: "It's a bit flattering," he says. "But it takes away from the uniqueness when you no longer feel like you're doing something that's different from what everybody else is doing. Now it feels like I'm lost in a pile. That style is saturated. I'm very flattered by the imitation, but it feels like someone has stolen my toys. [*laughs*] 'Gimme my ball back, I'm going home!' "

JEFF BECK

Album: *Guitar Shop*
Studio: Sol Studio, England
Producers: Jeff Beck and Leif Mases

When Jeff Beck released *Guitar Shop* back in 1989, guitar-dominated instrumental albums by the likes of Steve Vai and Joe Satriani dwelled at the top of the charts. But instead of shredding over mile-a-minute beats like his counterparts, Beck eased off the accelerator and shifted down into cruising grooves, opting to dazzle listeners with unusual tones, unconventional licks and unbelievable whammy bar bends. *Guitar Shop* may not have had the commercial appeal of Beck's previous instrumental efforts *Blow By Blow* and *Wired*, but it showed that he was still both an innovator and a consummate musician.

Beck chose not to go with his usual Marshalls when recording

Guitar Shop, opting instead for a pair of Eighties Fender combos—a Princeton Reverb II and a Twin. "The combination of both amps was killer," says Beck. "I don't know what it was. The Princeton took care of tonal qualities that the other amp didn't have. It has an overload channel, so you can get midrange distortion. I tried recording using just the Twin, but without the Princeton the sound vanished. Leif [*Mases, recording engineer*] noticed it right away and said, 'The sound isn't as good. You've got to put the Princeton back on.' "

According to Mases, Beck used two pairs of Princetons and Twins. "We had one of each in the control room and one of each in the studio," he explains. "At times we would use the ones in the control room as heads and the ones in the studio as speakers. Other times we split the signal and used the control room amps as monitors, especially if we wanted to generate feedback."

Beck plugged into his stage setup occasionally, which consisted of a late-Sixties Marshall 50-watt head. A Rat distortion pedal and a Boss DD-2 Digital Delay. He played several Strats and Teles, including prototypes for his Fender Strat signature model equipped with Lace Sensor pickups and a Wilkinson roller nut that helped him stay in tune while he executed the otherworldly whammy bar work on "Where Were You."

Even with such a small setup, Beck was able to create a vast array of sounds. The secret, says Mases, is Beck himself. "Jeff is an instrumentalist, but he isn't into equipment. His sound comes from his fingers more than anything. He gets a variety of sounds through his playing, and he can sound like himself no matter what equipment he's using. He's a true master of the instrument."

THE WHO'S PETE TOWNSHEND

Album: *Who's Next*
Studio: Olympic, London
Producers: The Who and Glyn Johns

Standing before a wall of Hiwatt amplifiers, bashing and eventually trashing his Gibson SGs and Les Pauls, Pete Townshend cast a lasting impression of rock and roll fury onstage with the Who in the Seventies. But when recording *Who's Next*, the landmark album that contains show-stopping classics such as "Won't Get Fooled Again" and "Baba

O'Riley," Townshend cast aside his stage setup and plugged into an unlikely Gretsch guitar/Fender amp combination previously associated with hillbilly crooners and rockabilly artists like Eddie Cochran.

His main setup for the album—a 1957 Gretsch 6120 guitar, a late-Fifties tweed Fender Bandmaster amp and an Edwards volume pedal—was a gift from Joe Walsh. "I had given Joe an ARP 2600 synthesizer," Townshend recalls. "A few months later he called me and said, 'Pete, I didn't know what to get you in return, but I bought you a Gretsch like Neil Young uses. I know you're not really into them, but you should try this. And I bought you a Fender Bandmaster amplifier with three 10-inch speakers and an Edwards pedal steel volume pedal.' I linked it all up, went 'Ya-a-a-ang,' and it was magical. Whenever I get those three things out and hook them up together, it's a sound from paradise."

Townshend used this setup to record most of *Who's Next* and the Who's subsequent album, *Quadrophenia.* Unlike Pete's stage equipment, which the guitarist often transformed into sawdust, toothpicks and confetti by the end of a performance, he's hung onto and treasured this combination, even if he hasn't exactly pampered it. "I've still got the Gretsch," says Townshend, "although it got broken by accident when I trod on it. I fixed it up and it still sounds wonderful. I often use the same chain, even the exact same guitar cable—an old Whirlwind—when I'm recording. But if you try to fuck with the setup—for instance, play the Gretsch through a Zoom pedal—it doesn't work. It's got to be that exact combination of stuff. There are lots of setups that produce great sounds. This is ancient wisdom. Seek and ye shall find."

PANTERA'S DIMEBAG DARRELL

Album: *Far Beyond Driven*
Studio: Pantego Studios, Nashville
Producers: Terry Date and Vinnie Paul

Pantera's 1994 *Far Beyond Driven* album is graced with the band's raunchiest riffs, rudest lyrics and rawest tones. According to guitarist Dimebag Darrell, the especially obnoxious performance had more to do with the band's attitude than any special studio techniques or secret processors.

"We're into doing new stuff," says Dime. "We got together, had a good time, drank some beer, smoked some weed and wrote some songs. We had a vision, and that's all it took."

Dimebag used the same rig that he uses live for recording. "I had three Randall half-stacks in the studio," he comments. "I love the sound of those solid-state Randalls. I don't want no warm sound. I ain't lookin' for a soft sound. Solid-state is more in your face than tubes. My Randall's got the warmth of the tubes, but it's got the chunk and the fuckin' grind right in your face."

Dime's main ax for most of *Far Beyond Driven* was his favorite blue Dean ML, outfitted with Bill Lawrence 500 XL pickups and a Floyd Rose tremolo. "It's on all the songs that are in regular standard tuning—except we drop down a couple cents from standard," he explains. "My tobacco-burst Dean is on the songs where the whole guitar is tuned down a whole step or more. I experimented with different string gauges for the album—went from .046s to .048s to .050s, checkin' out the chunk. My La Bella Hard Rockin' Steels have quite a bit to do with my tone. They're real brassy sounding."

Dimebag doubles most of his rhythm guitar tracks. During mixing, the parts are panned to the left and right channels to give the guitar sound more punch. "They're not panned hard left and right, but just a little off of that, about three o'clock and nine o'clock," says Dime. "I'd be done as soon as the drum track's done if I didn't prefer the thickness of a doubled guitar sound, but that's my tone." "Throes of Rejection" and "Hard Lines, Sunken Cheeks" feature three-part harmonies, and sometimes Dime added a third rhythm part which was panned to the center.

"That's as thick as it got," he says. "I didn't go overboard. Whenever I start to layer more than two or three guitars it gets cluttered up, and you can't hear the cut of the guitar as good because it's hard to make three or four guitars hit at exactly the same time. It clutters up the attack. I have to play within certain boundaries, but I don't want it too tight. Too tight is sterile. Too loose is too sloppy."

Dime added a few new tone toys to his audio arsenal prior to recording, most notably a DigiTech Whammy Pedal that can be heard on "Strength Beyond Strength" and "Becoming." "For 'Becoming' I had the Whammy Pedal set at two octaves," he notes. "I was playing octaves, and I fuckin' hopped on the pedal when I popped that note."

AC/DC's
ANGUS AND MALCOLM YOUNG
Album: *Ballbreaker*
Studio: Ocean Way, Los Angeles
Producers: Rick Rubin and AC/DC

The classic AC/DC crunch has thrived throughout the years with little variation and absolutely no dilution of its 100-proof kick. Why tamper with perfection? Sometime during their teen years in Australia, brothers Angus and Malcolm Young concocted the right formula. Malcolm holds down rhythm on his customized '63 Gretsch Jet Firebird while Angus cuts loose on a Gibson SG. For AC/DC's 1995 *Ballbreaker* album, the Brothers Young honed their timeless guitar formula to a razor-sharp edge.

"We went through all the old Marshalls in our warehouses in London and took our time picking out the best ones," says Angus.

Longtime AC/DC guitar technician Alan Rogan elaborates: "We had a pile of Marshall amps, but for Malcolm, it boiled down to a 100-watt plexi '66. In fact, it might even be a '65—it has a hand-bent aluminum chassis. He used this with a Marshall cab loaded with 25-watt Greenbacks. Besides his guitar, that was it—no effects. For Angus we narrowed it down to three JTM-45 plexi heads: one for the track, one for the power chords [*overdubbed embellishments*] and one for solos. And there weren't many power chord tracks. For the rhythm tracks, the head went through a Marshall cabinet with Vintage 30 Celestions. But for solos, we bought an old Marshall basket-weave cabinet and put new Greenbacks in—same as Malcolm."

Guitarwise, Angus mainly played a '64 Gibson SG, although he occasionally used two '68 SGs. Both brothers use Fender extra-heavy picks. And for *Ballbreaker*, Rogan even tracked down some old sets of heavy Gibson Sonomatic strings (.012–.056) that Malcolm swore by in the early days. The rest was sheer testosterone.

NIRVANA'S KURT COBAIN

Album: *Nevermind*
Studios: Sound City, Van Nuys; Devonshire, North Hollywood
Producers: Butch Vig and Nirvana

The watery depths of open-string anguish, the toxic mixture of wattage plus aggression...Kurt Cobain's guitar sound on Nirvana's *Nevermind* set the tone for Nineties rock music. The basic elements of this potent formula were simple. Cobain's axes for the *Nevermind* session were a late-Sixties Mustang, a Jaguar with DiMarzio pickups and several new Stratocasters with humbuckers in the bridge positions. His principal effects were a Boss DS-1 distortion pedal and an Electro-Harmonix Small Clone Chorus, and his main amp was a Mesa/Boogie Studio .22. Producer Butch Vig recalls, "We also had a Fender Bassman that he used on about four songs and a Vox AC30 that we did some clean tracks with. I basically recorded the band live, and then we went back and doubled some rhythm guitars and overdubbed some riffs and other things."

Vig used four mikes on Cobain's speaker cabinet: a Shure SM-57, a Neumann U87, an AKG 414 and, occasionally, a Sennheiser 421. For any given song he'd select the best-sounding mic of the four and send its signal through the Neve console at Sound City. The aforementioned Small Clone, says Vig, was the key to "the watery guitar sound you hear on the pre-chorus build-up of 'Smells Like Teen Spirit' and also 'Come As You Are.' I believe we also used a ProCo Rat distortion pedal on some songs. We used an Electro-Harmonix Big Muff fuzz box through a Fender Bassman amp on 'Lithium,' to get that thumpier, darker sound. As I recall, we used a U87 mic on that. We wanted something that was not so bright—a heavier sound."

Although it's not credited on the album, the acoustic song "Polly" was recorded at Vig's own Smart Studios in Madison, Wisconsin, during demo sessions for *Nevermind*. Cobain recorded "Polly" using a very cheap no-name acoustic that had just five strings. "He'd never changed the guitar's strings," Vig recalls. "It was tuned about a step and a half down from E. I recorded it with an AKG 414. The same guitar is on 'Something in the Way.' "

JIMI HENDRIX

Song: "All Along the Watchtower"
Studios: Olympic, London; Record Plant, New York
Producer: Jimi Hendrix

Jimi Hendrix's recording of Bob Dylan's apocalyptic masterpiece was one of many high points on the Experience's *Electric Ladyland* LP, not to mention the group's only Top 20 hit. The events of the historic tracking session in London's Olympic Studios, on January 21, 1968, have been well documented. Hendrix's friend Dave Mason, of the group Traffic, had been drafted to play acoustic guitar, but kept stumbling over the chord progression, causing Experience bassist Noel Redding to lose patience and seek the solace of a nearby pub. The four-track rhythm bed was cut without any bass, with Mason on acoustic, Hendrix on electric and Mitch Mitchell on drums. The electric guitar sound was generated by Hendrix's classic Strat-into-Marshall rig.

"Hendrix's setup for that song was fairly straight-ahead," recalls session engineer Eddie Kramer. "He used few, if any, effects. The amp wasn't cranked very loudly. He was absolutely the master of getting a clean sound out of that Strat and Marshall."

Kramer further recollects that "the room at Olympic was huge—about 70 feet by 45 feet by 45 feet high. Jimi's amps were set in the middle of the room." The engineer says he mixed only one of Hendrix's cabinets: a 4 x 12 Marshall slant cab powered by a 100-watt Marshall head. Kramer refuses to disclose the mic that he used to capture Jimi's immortal guitar sound on that track, saying that everyone will have to wait until the publication of his forthcoming book to find out. However, he reveals that "the reverb was the key to the whole thing. Olympic's EMT [*reverb*] plate had an absolutely gorgeous sound."

Some of the track's tenebrous tone is attributable to good-old analog tape generation loss from transferring the tracks to several machines. "After we cut the basic tracks—stereo drums, acoustic guitar and Jimi's electric—I mixed that down to two tracks on another four-track machine," Kramer recounts, "and we put on Jimi's bass and vocal. Then we mixed that down to another four-track, leaving room for the percussion. [*Including the vibraslap that is one of the song's sonic signatures.*] It had already gone two or three generations down by the time the tape was transferred to a Scully 12-track machine at the Record Plant in New York."

Hendrix overdubbed extensively on "All Along the Watchtower." No one is certain when the master axman laid down each part of his memorable solo on the track, which includes some beautifully echoed and panned passages created with one of Hendrix's Roger Mayer-modified Cry Baby wah-wah pedals. Eddie Kramer believes that all the leads went down live at Olympic, but can't say for sure. Like the identity of Dylan's two approaching riders, some things will always remain a mystery."

Metallica's JAMES HETFIELD

Album: *Live Shit: Binge and Purge*
Producers: James Hetfield and Lars Ulrich

Metallica's 1988 masterpiece, *...And Justice for All,* may not have won any "best production" Grammys for its dry-as-a-bone mix, but it established the band as a chart-topping, stadium-filling entity, and it did so without compromising the band's unique style in any way. Their tour in support of this album is documented on the 1993 *Live Shit: Binge and Purge* double CD/triple video box set collection.

Live Shit proved beyond doubt that James Hetfield is thrash/speed metal's preeminent rhythm player. Even without the benefit of studio trickery such as multiple punch-ins and multilayered parts, Hetfield delivered 100 percent ultra hi-gain, "scooped" (lots of lows and highs, no mids) rhythm tone. His sound is crunchy as hell, yet tight and well defined with a bottom so full and fat it completely cloaks the bass guitar. In fact, if it weren't for Jason Newsted's likeness appearing on the package, you'd swear the band didn't have a bassist!

Hetfield's guitars for the *...And Justice for All* tour were four ESP Explorers loaded with EMG pickups and strung with Ernie Ball RPS strings (.010, .013, .017, .026, .036, .046). He used a variety of amps and preamps for different tones, including a Mesa/Boogie Simul-Class II amp and ADA MP-1 preamp for his main rhythm tone and a Roland JC-120 combo and a Mesa/Boogie Studio preamp for clean sounds. The amps were connected to 280-watt Marshall 1960BV 4 x 12 cabinets. Several effects processors were integral to his sound as well, including a Boss SE-50, BBE Sonic Maximizer, Rocktron Juice

Extractor, Aphex parametric EQ and Hush noise reduction. Hetfield controlled his rack with a Bradshaw switching system.

The most crucial aspect of Hetfield's rig—his tone settings—has remained a closely guarded secret to this day. However, it is widely known that he preferred a "scooped-mid" setting where essentially all of the midrange is cut and the high and low EQ is boosted. Since this groundbreaking era, James' dark and evil tone hasn't lost any of its face-ripping edge, but it has changed somewhat in that all-important, mid-frequency area: "What happened was I discovered that midrange is, well, loud!" Hetfield revealed shortly after the release of the multi-Platinum *Metallica* in 1991. "I used to turn my amp's mid-control all the way counterclockwise and then tape it there. Now I've gotten rid of the tape."

The Sex Pistols' STEVE JONES

Song: "Anarchy in the U.K."
Studio: Wessex, London
Producer: Chris Thomas

Vicious rumors and strange legends surround Steve Jones' huge guitar sound on the Sex Pistols' first official single, which became a key track on the revolution-inciting *Never Mind the Bollocks (Here's the Sex Pistols)*. Did Jones really play on the record, or was it Chris Spedding? Are there really 21 tracks of guitar on there?

Jones maintains that he played all the guitar parts on "Anarchy." Jones says he used one of two Gibson Les Pauls he owned at the time: a white one that once belonged to Syl Sylvain of the New York Dolls and a black one that the guitarist called his "Black Beauty," in homage to a particular type of amphetamine he favored back then. And while many people assume that the powerhouse guitar sound on "Anarchy" came from a Marshall amp, Jones says it was actually a Fender Twin Reverb that he "stole off Bob Marley at the Hammersmith Odeon [*a theater in London*]. It was a real old one—a Silverface [*which Fender started manufacturing in '68*]. It didn't have the pull-out switch. I put Gauss speakers in it, which took away the real trebly sound and gave it a lot of midrange. It was fuckin' awesome—a nice warm sound, but it had a lot of distortion. You had to have it turned up to 10 the whole time. It just had this one sound, but it was killer."

on Savage's book, *England's Dreaming*, Johnny Rotten complains that there were 21 guitar overdubs on "Anarchy," which left only one track for the vocals. Jones dismisses this as, well, bollocks: "There's mainly two tracks of guitar doing the rhythm with some kind of flange or phase on it. Then there's a third track of guitar playing chords here and there, but not throughout the whole song. Like, after one chorus, another guitar will come in playing open chords. There's a track with guitar doing a feedback thing near the end, and there's one doing power chords at the end. I'd say there were about six tracks of guitar in all, which is a far cry from 21."

Leading Men

A Slew of Guitar Giants Weigh In on Their Favorite Solos

EDWARD VAN HALEN

Favorite Solo: "I'm So Glad" by Eric Clapton
Album: *Cream–Goodbye* (Polydor, 1969)

"Here's Clapton literally blowing jazz through a Marshall stack for almost 10 minutes, and it's all amazing."

KIRK HAMMETT (Metallica)

Favorite Solo: "Machine Gun" by Jimi Hendrix
Album: *Jimi Hendrix–Band of Gypsys* (Experience Hendrix, 1970)

"The thing that attracts me, other than the incredible playing, is that he tuned down almost to C#, which gives the whole track so much weight. For years, I couldn't figure out what he was doing. There's just so much drama on that track. Every time I hear it, it just kills me."

MARK KNOPFLER (Dire Straits)

Favorite Solo: "Hound Dog" by Scotty Moore
Album: *Elvis Presley–Top Ten Hits* (RCA, 1987)

"The second solo says it all about rock and roll guitar playing. It's just wild, with this great big banging and cracking going on. I've asked Scotty about it and he doesn't know how he did it. It just happened. For something more modern, I'd pick Jimi Hendrix's 'Hey Joe,' which is just beautiful and has a tremendous intro as well."

DIMEBAG DARRELL (PANTERA)

Favorite Solo: "Revelation (Mother Earth)" by Randy Rhoads
Album: Ozzy Osbourne–*Blizzard of Ozz* (Epic, 1981)

"God-damn, brother! If you love listening to guitar playing, how are you gonna answer that question? There's millions of great ones! Right here, right now, 'Revelation (Mother Earth),' off *Blizzard of Ozz*, is ringing out pretty hard. The whole structure behind it is very cool and I love that mode it's in—that Egyptian-sounding shit or whatever it is."

BILLY GIBBONS (ZZ TOP)

Favorite Solo: "Stormy Monday Blues" by Wayne Bennett
Album: Bobby "Blue" Bland–*Turn on Your Love Light* (MCA, 1994)

"Impeccable tone, taste and tricks of time, all wrapped up in 12 bars. What else do you need?"

BUDDY GUY

Favorite Solo: "Ten Long Years" by B.B. King
Album: B.B. King–My Sweet Little Angel (Flair/Virgin, 1992)

"The playoff between B.B.'s guitar and the horns during the solo were very inspiring to me."

JOE SATRIANI

Favorite Solo: "Voodoo Child (Slight Return)" by Jimi Hendrix
Album: Jimi Hendrix Experience–*Electric Ladyland* (Experience Hendrix/MCA, 1968)

"It is just the greatest piece of electric guitar work ever recorded. In fact, the whole song could be considered the holy grail of guitar expression and technique. It is a beacon of humanity."

STEVE VAI

Favorite Solo: "Heartbreaker" by Jimmy Page
Album: Led Zeppelin–*Led Zeppelin II* (Atlantic, 1969)

"This one had the biggest impact on me as a youth. It was defiant, bold and edgier than hell. It really is the definitive rock guitar solo."

KERRY KING (SLAYER)

Favorite Solo: "Beyond the Realms of Death" by Glenn Tipton
Album: Judas Priest–*Stained Class* (Columbia, 1978)

"I don't even have to think about that! It's a fantastic lead and I think Tipton is one of rock's most underrated players. That solo is brimming with emotion. It's like a guitar school on record, and that's where I studied."

JEFF HANNEMAN (SLAYER)

Favorite Solo: "Rock Bottom" by Michael Schenker
Album: UFO–*Strangers in the Night* (Chrysalis, 1979)

"That solo always stuck with me because it was just so long and moody. I dug the way it would change from being real melodic to real aggressive."

DAVE MUSTAINE (MEGADETH)

Favorite Solo: "Shine On You Crazy Diamond" by David Gilmour
Album: Pink Floyd—*Wish You Were Here* (Columbia, 1975)

"David Gilmour can do more with one note than most guitar players can do with the whole fretboard."

RITCHIE BLACKMORE

Favorite Solo: "Believe What You Say" by James Burton
Album: Ricky Nelson—*Legendary Masters* (EMI, 1990)

"It sounded like there were four guitars playing and it was just so emotional. It was one of the first ones I really heard and it made me want to play guitar, along with the solo on Buddy Holly's 'It's So Easy.' "

MIKE STERN

Favorite Solo: "Them Changes" by Jimi Hendrix
Album: Jimi Hendrix—*Band of Gypsys* (Experience Hendrix, 1970)

"I love the way Jimi played with time. He's so slinky over the beats and on the live *Band of Gypsys*, he stretches out and it's so raw. In a jazzier vein, Jim Hall's performance of 'My Funny Valentine' [*Undercurrent* (Blue Note, 1962)] has every element of a great solo: the touch is incredible, the content is great, the development is phenomenal and the feel is fantastic."

TREY ANASTASIO (PHISH)

Favorite Solo: "Machine Gun" by Jimi Hendrix
Album: Jimi Hendrix—*Band of Gypsys* (Experience Hendrix, 1970)

"Not only is this my favorite guitar solo all the time, but it also includes the greatest single note ever played on electric guitar, which is the high, screaming note Jimi plays right after the verse ends. That hanging note is the deepest, most intense note I've ever heard. I've loved that solo and record since I was in ninth grade, and it's never been matched for me."

WARREN HAYNES (GOV'T MULE)

Favorite Solo: "All Along the Watchtower" by Jimi Hendrix
Album: Jimi Hendrix Experience–*Electric Ladyland* (Experience Hendrix, 1968)

"The whole thing is magical, from beginning to end, and is the perfect example of what you can do in the studio."

MAX CAVALERA (SOULFLY)

Favorite Solo: "Africa Unite" by Julian "Junior" Marvin
Album: Bob Marley and the Wailers–*Survival* (Tuff Gong, 1979)

"It's one of my favorite solos because of its simplicity—but it adds so much to the song. 'Africa Unite' is definitely one of Marley's finest moments. Great stuff."

TED NUGENT

Favorite Soloist: Chuck Berry
Album: Chuck Berry–*Chess Box* (Chess, 1988)

"If you don't know every Chuck Berry lick, you can't play rock guitar."

AL DI MEOLA

Favorite Solo: "Giant Steps" by John Coltrane
Album: John Coltrane–*Giant Steps* (Atlantic, 1959)

"This saxophone composition has long been, and most likely will always be, the most exciting solo for me, on any instrument, due to its constant harmonic changes and the tempo at which it is played."

PHIL COLLEN (DEF LEPPARD)

Favorite Solo: "Highway Star" by Ritchie Blackmore
Album: Deep Purple–*Machine Head* (Warner Bros., 1972)

"When I first started off playing, that was kind of a blueprint for what I was trying to do as a soloist. It has great technique, great vibrato and great melody—it's spot on."

STEPHEN CARPENTER (DEFTONES)

Favorite Solo: "Dirty Movies" by Edward Van Halen
Album: Van Halen–*Fair Warning* (Warner Bros., 1981)

"The best soloing I've ever heard is on Van Halen's *Fair Warning*. Ed's playing on the whole album is non-stop melody. He's not just ripping, he's totally tasteful on every song."

VIVIAN CAMPBELL (DEF LEPPARD)

Favorite Solo: "Mean Street" by Edward Van Halen
Album: Van Halen–*Fair Warning* (Warner Bros., 1981)

"It's a Van Halen solo—surprise, surprise! The reason I like that solo so much is that it is just so lyrical and expressive while having a lot of tension. Ed applies his liquid-like magic, but the whole structure of the solo is very dynamic."

SLASH

Favorite Solo: "Dead Flowers" by Mick Taylor
Album: Rolling Stones–*Sticky Fingers* (Virgin, 1971)

"Sometimes you'll just be listening to something while you're sweeping up the room or brushing your teeth that'll make you stop and pay attention. It might be texture in a guitar solo, note choice or tone, whatever… And that's what happened to me this morning with Mick Taylor's solo in that particular song."

RICH ROBINSON (BLACK CROWES)

Favorite Solo: "The Fan" by Lowell George
Album: Little Feat–*Feats Don't Fail Me Now* (Warner Bros., 1974)

"It has true feel—an area where Lowell always shined—and melodic sense for days."

NANCY WILSON (HEART)

Favorite Solo: "I'm Only Sleeping" by George Harrison
Album: The Beatles–*Revolver* (Capitol, 1966)

"It's impossible, of course, to choose only one favorite guitar solo because it requires you to neglect too many unforgettable moments of sheer guitar rapture and bliss, like David Gilmour on 'Wish You Were Here,' Jimmy Page on 'You Shook Me' or Eric Clapton on 'Strange Brew.' But there's one way to narrow it down—put the problem to the hootenany test. To decide who wins, you need to count how many people in a jam-in-the-living-room situation can actually *sing* the guitar solo because it's such a fundamental part of the song. I recently conducted such a test and the hands-down winner was the backward guitar solo in the early Beatles song 'I'm Only Sleeping.' Remember? That's the one that goes, 'Reeeoooooooooo deer deer deer duhdul doodul dreer do do dweet!' "

SCOTT IAN (ANTHRAX)

Favorite Solo: "Sails of Charon" by Uli Jon Roth
Album: Scorpions–*Taken By Force* (RCA, 1978)

"It's the most perfect solo I've ever heard—it's super clean, it's super melodic, it tells a story and it's something that if I practiced for the rest of my life, I would never be able to play."

Guitar World, May 1998

Wah My Guitar Gently Weeps: A Lesson with Kirk Hammett

The Metallica guitarist examines the techniques and theoretical approach that have made him a hard rock legend.

Metallica's Kirk Hammett is a giant among men. There isn't a guitar poll he hasn't won, and his popularity runs high among fans and critics alike. Few would dispute the contention that he is, with the possible exception of Edward Van Halen, the most influential hard rock/metal lead guitarist alive today.

In keeping with Metallica's public disavowal of the "metal" label, the most recent *Guitar World* Readers Poll saw Hammett win the "Best Rock Guitarist" crown. In belated celebration of Kirk's latest triumph, *Guitar World* proudly presents an intimate look at his technique—as seen through the eyes of the guitarist himself.

...AND RHYTHM FOR ALL

James Hetfield, of course, is known as the rhythmic rock on which Metallica stands. As a result, Hammett begins the lesson by focusing on a side of his own playing for which he is perhaps underrated. "Although I'm a lead guitarist, I'd say that a good 95 percent of my time onstage is spent playing rhythm," says Hammett. "Consequently, it doesn't matter how great your lead playing is—if your rhythm work sucks, you're not gonna go very far. When you're playing rhythm in a band like Metallica, what your right [*picking*] hand does is really important. Obviously, what your left hand is doing is pretty darned crucial too, but, as a lot of our riffs involve syncopated open-string notes and relatively simple-to-finger power chords, it's often the right-hand picking and muting techniques that can make or break a song."

Mick Hutson/Retna

Kirk Hammett

KAPTAIN KRUNCH!

Before getting down to the nuts and bolts of his muting and picking, Hammett takes some time to dispel a few common misconceptions about his band's mighty rhythm tone. "The first thing I gotta say is that Metallica's crunch sound is often cleaner than people expect," he says. "Actually, to be honest, my taste in tone has definitely changed over the years—I don't like to use as much distortion these days, I prefer my tone to be nice and crisp. Don't get me wrong, distortion is great, but there's definitely a point where having too much turns your tone to mush—the low end loses its tightness and your overall tone gets flabby, with no definition or cut.

"When you're first starting out, there's always the temptation to hide behind distortion because it lets you get away with murder. But, when it comes to rhythm work, you've gotta back off that gain control a bit—especially if you're playing with another guitarist. Actually, over the years, James and I have found that besides giving our tone more definition and cut, backing off the gain makes us play our riffs better because we can't get away with being sloppy.

"Another thing a lot of people assume about Metallica's rhythm tone is that we scoop out all of the mid frequencies," continues Hammett. "Well, we used to do that, but while making *Metallica* [*1991*] we rediscovered midrange and how much louder and fuller our guitars sound with it in there."

THE POINT IS MUTE

"A lot of our riffs involve right-hand palm muting [*P.M.*]," says Hammett. "It's actually a pretty easy technique to master. Here are a couple of quick do's and don'ts:

1. To palm-mute a chord or note correctly, rest the lower part of your right palm on the strings right where they go over the bridge. Don't go too far away from the bridge, though, otherwise the notes will lose their definition and become dull thuds.
2. If you play a guitar with a fixed bridge—like a Les Paul or the ESP Explorer James uses—you can be pretty heavy handed when muting. If your guitar has a whammy system that's set up 'floating,' like mine is, so you can pull the bar up as well as push it down, you've gotta be a bit more careful, though. If you lean too hard on a floating bridge when you're palm-muting, you'll end up pushing the bridge down and sounding like shit because your strings will all go sharp."

UP ON THE DOWNSIDE

When performing many of Metallica's more brutal motifs, Hammett believes that, "to attain maximum heaviness, you've got to pick using downstrokes exclusively. It just sounds tighter, chunkier and more aggressive when you do that," he says. "It's important to be proficient at playing upstrokes too, because they have a different attack, and that can be useful sometimes. I can remember seeing old Deep Purple videos and noticing that Ritchie Blackmore picked upwards on a lot of his riffs."

Even those who are extremely adept at downpicking, notes Hammett, must observe a speed limit: "We play the intro to 'Master of Puppets' [*Master of Puppets*]—eighth notes at about 220 beats per minute—using all downstrokes. Although that tempo isn't our absolute limit, it's definitely getting there. As for a riff like the one at the beginning of 'Whiplash' [*Kill 'Em All*] [*16th notes at 160 b.p.m.*], alternate picking is a must!"

WRIST WATCH

"One thing I've noticed over the years," says Hammett, "is that there are basically two distinct approaches to picking: those who pick with their wrist and those who pick with their whole forearm. I've found that you have a lot more control over your picking when you pivot from your wrist, as opposed to pivoting from your elbow, because there's just less overall movement going on. By picking this way, you can fine tune your right hand technique into a very precise and controlled wrist maneuver. Basically, the smaller and more economical the movement, the better.

"Getting this picking approach down can really make a big difference—especially when you're playing a fast riff using all downstrokes. Also, when you pick by moving your forearm, it's a lot harder to palm-mute the strings by the bridge. When you pivot from your wrist, though, it's easy to get that palm-muted 'chunk' happening with your right hand because it's hardly moving."

To illustrate this particular picking approach, Hammett offered up the two simple practice exercises shown in **FIGURES 1** and **2**. "Because your fretboard hand isn't doing anything, you can totally zone in on ensuring that you're pivoting from your wrist and that your picking motion is as precise and economical as possible," says Hammett. "Start off slowly and then build up speed. Provided you're willing to spend some time working on them, these two exercises will help you build up the right-hand speed and stamina you need for intense, palm-muted, down-picked riffing."

Hammett points out that a mastery of downpicking brings with it some substantial fringe benefits. "A lot of my soloing involves downpicking," he points out. "Whenever I'm doing a bend, an artificial [*pinch*] harmonic, a pull-off or a hammer-on, I always attack the string using a downstroke. I also find that using mostly downstrokes in my leads gives me more attack and subtlety. It's easier to make a note, even if it's a harmonic, jump out when you downpick."

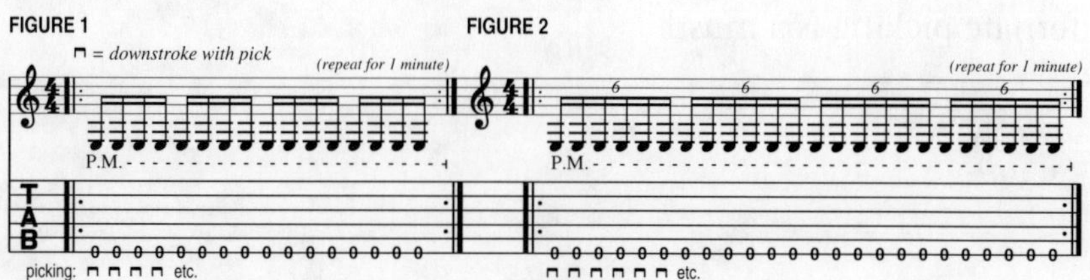

START ME UP

Hammett, a keen advocate of downpicking, is also pretty hot on the topic of warming up. Appropriately, the two simple picking drills shown in **FIGURES 1** and **2** also happen to be great warm-up exercises. "There is no 'right' way to warm up before a gig because everyone's approach is different," he says. "Some guitarists don't warm up at all, believing that they'll play better going out there fresh. I've always found that, in order to do my best, I have to warm up. While many players are concerned that if they don't warm up, they'll hurt their hands, I just worry about a different kind of pain—one that comes from the embarrassment of standing before an audience and being unable to play what I have to play! Hell, I even do a quick warm-up routine before I try something out in a music store!"

FIGURES 3 and **4** illustrate the ascending and descending versions of a warm-up exercise that Hammett picked up from a friend. "These two exercises are really good for developing coordination between your left and right hands," he says. "They're also cool because they cover the whole fretboard and require you to use all four left-hand fingers. Incidentally, if you don't use your pinkie, I recommend you start using it—it's there, so why not use it?" He adds, "When I first learned to play, someone told me, 'Hey, you'd better use your little finger. Otherwise, it's just gonna hang there.' I've used it ever since. It definitely helps me play certain wide-stretch things [*plays the E-minor pentatonic run in* ***FIGURE 5***] that I probably couldn't reach if I were just a three-fingered player."

FIGURE 4

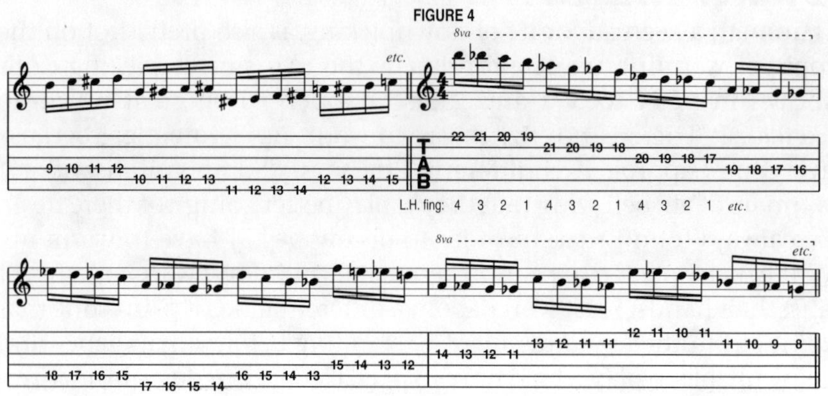

FIGURE 5

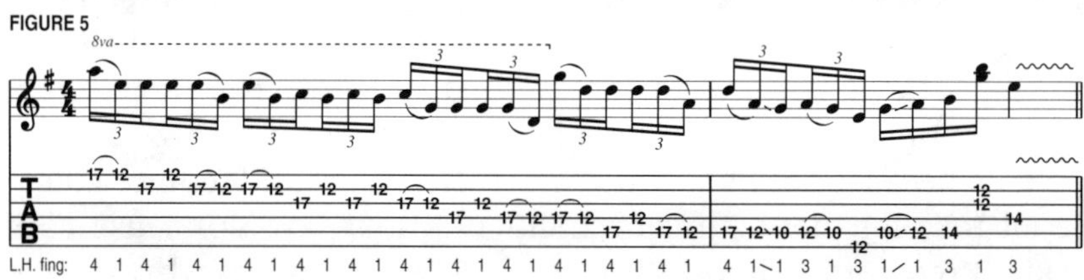

Hammett recommends using strict alternate picking (down, up, down, up, etc.) when performing **FIGURES 3** and **4**, and pivoting from the wrist, of course. "When it comes to playing fast, a lot of my colleagues only pick every third or fourth note and slur [*hammer-on, pull-off, bend, slide or tap*] the rest. Although I like the legato [*smooth*] feel you can get using hammer-ons and pull-offs, I think that you should be able to pick every note in a fast run if you want to be a well-rounded player. I've found that by picking virtually every note in a run, I have a lot more attack, and I can get more accents happening and convey percussive ideas, too."

SHAPE SHIFT: SHRED IS DEAD

Although quite capable of playing lightning-fast lead licks and runs, Hammett has not been doing much of that of late. When he first joined Metallica in the early Eighties, he was a self-described "shredder" and a pretty serious one at that, even taking lessons from the maestro, Joe Satriani. In the Nineties, however, Hammett's approach has become much more laid-back, even bluesy.

"Ten or 15 years ago, I was heavily into Uli Roth [*ex-Scorpions*] and all those contemporary 'shred' guitarists of the Eighties—you know, the Steve Vais and the Yngwie Malmsteens," he recalls. "But then, sometime around 1990, I just left that whole virtuoso thing behind. I basically decided, 'Screw what everyone around me is doing—from now on I'm just going to play what I think is important to me and to Metallica's music.' So I gave the big finger to all the technical wizardry trends and just went off and did what I felt was best for the songs. And, as it happens, a lot of the time, what's best for the song is often something relatively simple and bluesy. After all, the blues is all about tapping into your emotions."

Hammett's change of musical pace and approach is clearly reflected in the names of his current guitar heroes: Stevie Ray Vaughan, Johnny Winter, Eric Clapton, Buddy Guy, Jimmy Page, B.B. King, Freddie King and Warren Haynes. "In my opinion, these players can pack more of an emotional punch with a few bent notes than a lot of shredders can with oodles of 90-mile-per-hour scales.

"Though I still enjoy playing in a high-tech way every once in a while, nowadays I'm definitely more into space, sustain and tone—I'm always trying to work more space into my playing," says Hammett. "A lot of shredders don't seem to realize how space can be used constructively—they're just hell-bent on impressing you with how many notes they can fit in! To me, those players sound like they're hyperventilating musically. The reason shred earned such a bad rap is because so many guitarists didn't use technique tastefully or constructively. Remember, music isn't supposed to be pretentious.

"I tend to use speed as a texture nowadays," says Hammett. "Knowing when to play fast, when to play slow, and being able to mix it up makes all the difference in the world. There are some guitarists who basically play at one speed, and because of that their playing sounds flat and one-dimensional." He adds, "It's good to strive to be three-dimensional so that what you play has a lot of ups and downs, dips and so forth. You've got to let your playing breathe...you've got to let your tone breathe."

As a result of his "slow hand" approach, Hammett doesn't employ modes or exotic scales as much as he used to: "The major pentatonic [*see* ***FIGURE 6***] and minor pentatonic [*see* ***FIGURE 7***] are cool. They're the scales that I pretty much base my entire playing style on now."

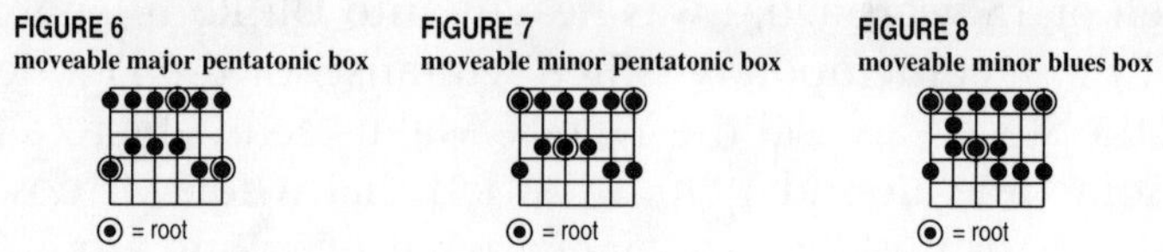

THE SPICE IS RIGHT

"Some people think that the only way to come up with new soloing ideas is to learn more scales," Hammett says disapprovingly. "I don't subscribe to that way of thinking because what the hell happens when you run out of scales and modes to learn? Anyhow, you don't have to know every exotic scale under the sun to come up with creative and exciting leads. I mean, there are only six notes within a standard minor-blues box [*see* ***FIGURE 8***], but there's so much you can do with them. I always find myself stumbling across different ways to spice up my well-worn blues licks—ways that are so unbelievably simple!"

Hammett proceeds to whip up a few examples of how to "spice up" an over-used blues lick. First he plays **FIGURES 9A** ("old"), then **9B** ("spiced-up"). "They're virtually the same exact A minor blues lick, except in the second one [***FIGURE 9B***] you bend up to the last note [G] from a semitone below [F#]. This very simple, subtle nuance," Hammett points out, "gives that final note a completely different type of vibrato sound and a crying, almost vocal quality that adds emotion to the lick."

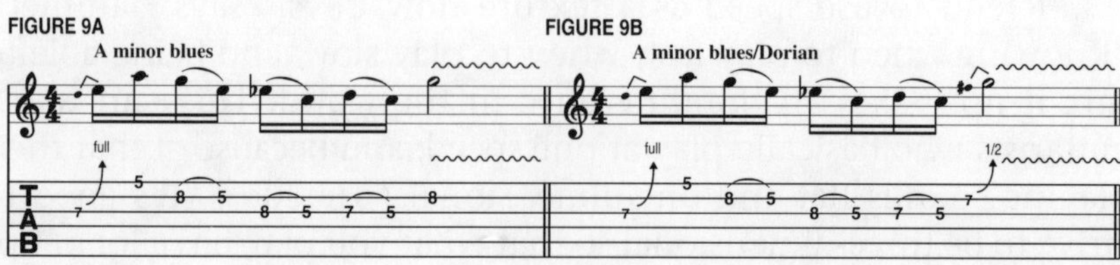

Now compare **FIGURES 10A** ("old") and **10B** ("spiced-up"), two versions of another blues lick, these in E minor pentatonic. The only difference between them, says Hammett, is that the "spiced-up" version has "a couple of trills and double-stops thrown in for extra excitement."

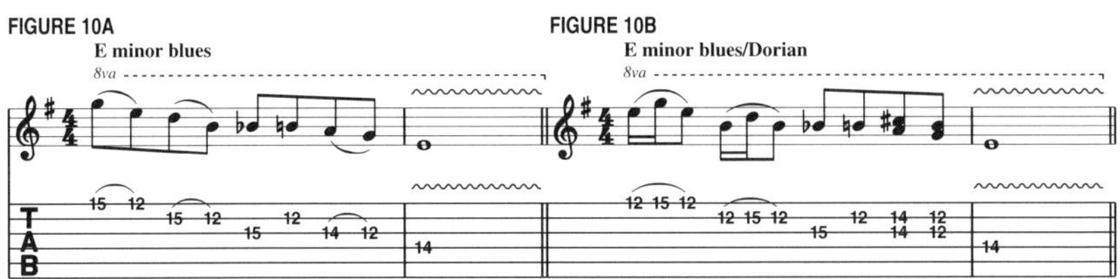

Here are several other easy, Kirk Hammett-approved ways to spice up your lead work:

1. **Use String Rakes:** This technique involves muting the strings marked with an "x" by lightly resting one of your left-hand fingers across them and then quickly dragging, or "raking," your pick across them, as indicated. "Kind of like percussive sweep picking," says Hammett with a grin, playing the C-minor pentatonic lick depicted in **FIGURE 11** to illustrate his point. "Doing this definitely adds extra emotion, attitude and emphasis to the initial string bend in this run. I do a lot of upstroke raking when I'm soloing, too." He demonstrates by playing the E-minor pentatonic lick shown in **FIGURE 12**. "I guess I got into this by listening to Ritchie Blackmore; he does it all the time."

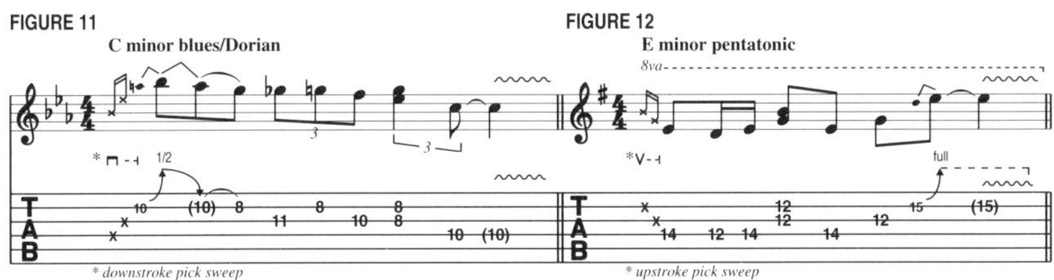

2. **Use Quarter-Tone Bends:** "One of the coolest things you can do to add bite and tension to a solo is bend certain notes just a tad so you're right in between two notes," says Hammett, playing the simple A-minor pentatonic lick shown in **FIGURE 13**. The quarter-tone bend occurs at the very beginning of bar 2. "Great blues players do this type of thing all the time. Stevie Ray Vaughan was especially good at it—he'd even add a quarter-tone bend to notes he'd already bent up by one or even two steps."

3. **Paraphrase**: "This is a great way of rejuvenating a tired old lick. The next time you find yourself guilty of recycling the same exact licks over and over, try taking a few of them and seeing how many different ways you can phrase them by merely altering the relative timing of each note and nothing else." To demonstrate this approach, Hammett plays the A-minor pentatonic motif illustrated in **FIGURE 14A** and then immediately rephrases it five different ways, as depicted in **FIGURES 14B-F**. "I realize this is an unbelievably basic concept, but most of the good ones are, and for that reason they're often overlooked," he says.

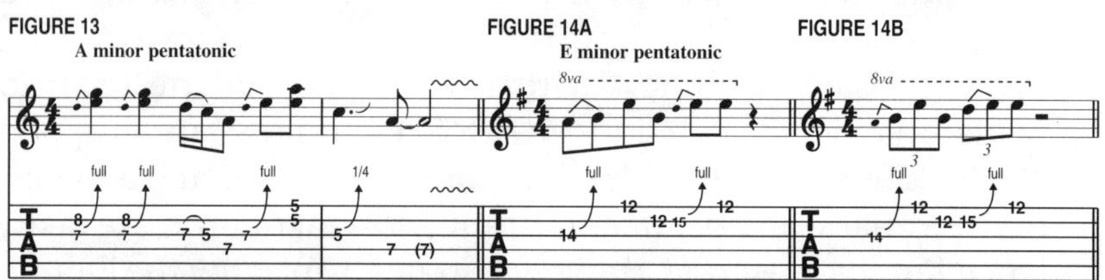

4. **Use String-Skipping and Wide Fretboard Stretches:** "Wide left-hand stretches and string-skipping can both open up new doors in your playing because each technique introduces you to intervals that you probably wouldn't normally use." **FIGURE 15** is a cool Hammett lick that hammers this point home by combining a five-fret stretch with some string-skipping. The result is "an Am7 arpeggio (A C E G) that will work in just about any A-minor context."

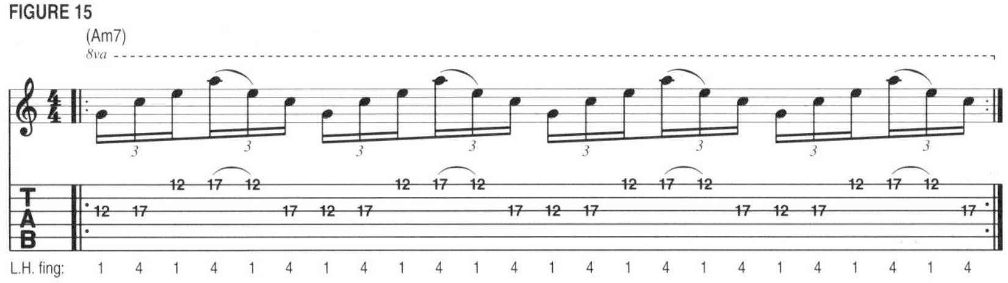

5. **Get a Wah-Wah Pedal:** "Every time I step on my wah-wah, it seems to kick-start my playing because its sound gives me instant inspiration. When the pedal is all the way down [*closed*], it gives me super aggression, and when it's all the way up [*open*], it adds a fluid coolness. Also, sweeping the thing through its complete range is a great way of accenting certain notes and phrases. I'm a total wah-wah freak—I think I'll die with one underneath my foot."

   Although he admires Jimi Hendrix's wah-wah use greatly, Hammett's biggest influence in this realm was a much less well-known player: "The guy who really turned my head around was Brian Robertson of Thin Lizzy," says Hammett. "He had a totally unique technique, and he made me realize that there are stylized ways of using the wah. Instead of using the pedal to accent individual notes, like most people do, Brian would do long, slow sweeps over a succession of notes to create and augment tension. His solo in "Opium Trail" [*Bad Reputation*] is a classic, and pretty much everything he did on Thin Lizzy's *Jailbreak* album is amazing, too.

   "There are a lot of great things you can do with a Crybaby Wah, and anyone who dismisses it as being a one-dimensional effect obviously hasn't looked or listened deeply enough. To me, the wah-wah is a tonal crayon you can use to color many aspects of your playing—and it's right there at your feet! I love this pedal to death. In fact, the only way you could keep me from playing one is by chopping off my legs!"

FIGURE 16 illustrates five of the many wah-wah phrasing approaches possible while simply ascending and descending the A minor pentatonic scale.

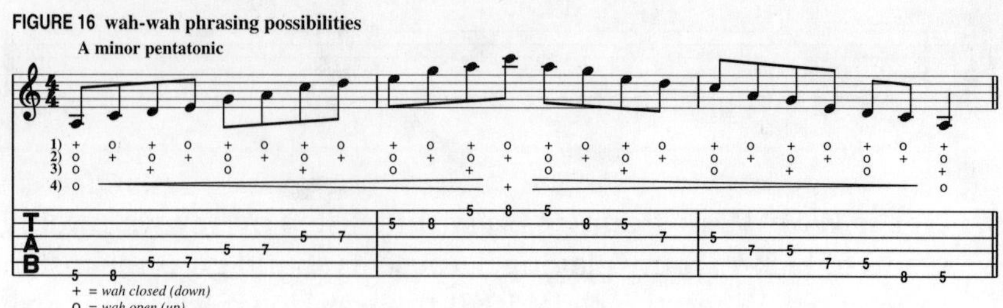

6. **Listen to Other Instruments:** "Listening to other instruments and then trying to copy their licks on guitar has definitely helped me expand my playing vocabulary," says Hammett. "There's nothing wrong with copying from other people, as long as you personalize what you copy. David Bowie once called himself *a very tasty thief*, and that's what you should aim to be. I've found that listening to and copying great jazz horn players opened up completely new horizons for me.

"If you're interested in getting into this type of stuff, two albums you must have are *Kind of Blue* by Miles Davis and John Coltrane's *Blue Train*. Although both of these guys play some mind-blowing, complex stuff, some of their greatest musical ideas are relatively simple." Hammett puts his money where his mouth is by playing **FIGURE 17**, an E-minor lick he "stole" from Coltrane. "It's unbelievably simple, but it's so percussive and melodic at the same time that it floors me every time I hear it."

7. **Listen Without Prejudice:** "I believe it's really important to listen to diverse forms of music, especially when you find yourself stuck in a playing rut. Don't cut yourself off from potentially great stuff by being narrow-minded. For example, not all country music sounds like Billy Ray Cyrus' "Achy Breaky Heart." Check out some of Albert Lee's work, for instance; he's an amazing guitarist in anyone's book. And what about the Allman Brothers? Their unique blend of country, blues and rock is unbelievable, and every guitarist can learn something from the late, great Duane Allman." To prove his point, Hammett plays **FIGURE 18**, "a string-skipping, E-major country blues lick inspired by listening to the Allmans' classic *At Fillmore East* album."

When performing **FIGURE 18**, Hammett sounded all the G-string notes with his pick while plucking the high E-string notes with his ring finger—a technique known as *hybrid picking*. "Doing this makes the run a lot easier to play because you don't have to worry about jumping over the B-string with your pick," he remarks. "Another neat thing about hybrid picking is that the notes you pick with your fingers have a slightly different tone and attack from those you hit with your pick."

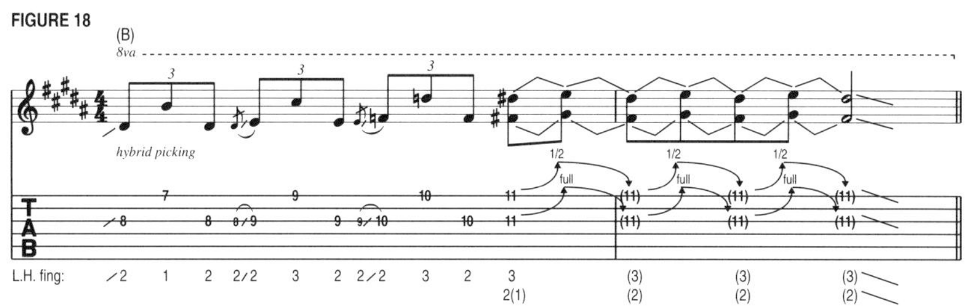

SOLO M.O.

Our look at Kirk Hammett's style wouldn't be complete without some concrete suggestions from the man on how to approach a lead break. "Although I don't have any set game plan for my solos, I'm totally from the school which says, 'Start out with a great idea, introduce a second great idea, resolve it and then end with a bang.' I always strive to have an intro, a mid-section and an end. When I have those things, I usually just improvise in between them. I also try to make every note count. Basically, I believe that a solo is a song within a song, and that's definitely how I feel when I'm working on a solo—I feel like I'm composing a song."

FINAL THOUGHTS

Hammett, a lighthearted sort except when it comes to guitar playing, closes his discourse with some deeply felt words he directs at all guitarists, all musicians. "Learn as much as you can, but when it comes down to the moment, throw it all out the window and play from inside yourself. I think that playing what you feel at the moment is really important. It doesn't matter if you know a billion scales or just two—trying to capture that emotion and trying to put it across is the name of the game. As far as I'm concerned, if you manage to channel your feelings through your playing—and whoever is listening understands the message—then you've succeeded as a musician.

"To achieve this goal, you've basically got to be yourself and try to be more fluid with your feelings. You shouldn't use scales as the middle man between your heart and your fingers, because sometimes that knowledge can be a barrier to what you really want to say. If you can eliminate that middle man, and just have a constant thought process that flows from your heart, through your fingers and out of your amp, that's the whole battle won right there."

PRESENTS

Guitar World Presents is an ongoing series of books filled with extraordinary interviews, feature pieces and instructional material that have made *Guitar World* magazine the world's most popular musicians' magazine. For years, *Guitar World* has brought you the most timely, the most accurate and the most hard-hitting news and views about your favorite players. Now you can have it all in one convenient package: *Guitar World Presents*.

Guitar World Presents Alternative Rock
00330369 (352 pages, 6" x 9")........................$17.95

Guitar World Presents Classic Rock
00330370 (288 pages, 6" x 9")........................$17.95

Guitar World Presents Kiss
00330291 (144 pages, 6" x 9")........................$14.95

Guitar World Presents Nü Metal
00330820 (160 pages, 6" x 9")........................$14.95

Guitar World Presents Pink Floyd
00330799 (144 pages, 6" x 9")........................$14.95

Guitar World Presents 100 Greatest Guitarists
00330960 (224 pages, 6" x 9")........................$16.95

Guitar World Presents Nirvana and the Grunge Revolution
00330368 (208 pages, 6" x 9")........................$16.95

Guitar World Presents Metallica
00330292 (144 pages, 6" x 9")........................$14.95

Guitar World Presents Van Halen
00330294 (208 pages, 6" x 9")........................$14.95

Guitar World Presents Stevie Ray Vaughan
00330293 (144 pages, 6" x 9")........................$14.95

FOR MORE INFORMATION, SEE YOUR LOCAL MUSIC DEALER, OR WRITE TO:

7777 W. BLUEMOUND RD. P.O. BOX 13819 MILWAUKEE, WI 53213

Prices and availability subject to change without notice.
Some products may not be available outside the U.S.A.